W9-CIJ-932

OPPOSING
VIEWPOINTS®
SERIES

The Future of Space Exploration

WITHDRAWN

Other Books of Related Interest

Opposing Viewpoints Series

Artificial Intelligence and the Technological Singularity
Global Sustainability
The Impact of Tech Giants
Space Exploration

At Issue Series

Adaptation and Climate Change
Space Exploration
What Is the Impact of Tourism?
Will the World Run out of Fresh Water?

Current Controversies Series

Conserving the Environment
The Global Food Crisis
Immigration
The World Economy

"Congress shall make
no law … abridging
the freedom of speech,
or of the press."

First Amendment to the US Constitution

The basic foundation of our democracy is the First Amendment guarantee of freedom of expression. The Opposing Viewpoints series is dedicated to the concept of this basic freedom and the idea that it is more important to practice it than to enshrine it.

OPPOSING
VIEWPOINTS®
SERIES

The Future of Space Exploration

Avery Elizabeth Hurt, Book Editor

GREENHAVEN
PUBLISHING

Published in 2020 by Greenhaven Publishing, LLC
353 3rd Avenue, Suite 255, New York, NY 10010

Copyright © 2020 by Greenhaven Publishing, LLC

First Edition

All rights reserved. No part of this book may be reproduced in any form
without permission in writing from the publisher, except by a reviewer.

Articles in Greenhaven Publishing anthologies are often edited for length to meet page
requirements. In addition, original titles of these works are changed to clearly present
the main thesis and to explicitly indicate the author's opinion. Every effort is made to
ensure that Greenhaven Publishing accurately reflects the original intent of the authors.
Every effort has been made to trace the owners of the copyrighted material.

Cover image: Vadim Sadovski/Shutterstock.com

Library of Congress Cataloging-in-Publication Data

Names: Hurt, Avery Elizabeth, compiler, editor.
Title: The future of space exploration / Avery Elizabeth Hurt, book editor,
[compiling editor].
Other titles: Opposing viewpoints series (Unnumbered)
Description: First edition. | New York : Greenhaven Publishing, 2020. |
Series: Opposing viewpoints | Audience: Grades 9 to 12. | Includes
bibliographical references and index.
Identifiers: LCCN 2018052895| ISBN 9781534505025 (library bound) | ISBN
9781534505032 (pbk.)
Subjects: LCSH: Astronautics—United States—Juvenile literature. | Outer
space—Exploration—Government policy—Juvenile literature. | Outer
space—Exploration—Public opinion—Juvenile literature.
Classification: LCC TL782.5 .H87 2020 | DDC 629.40973—dc23
LC record available at https://lccn.loc.gov/2018052895

Manufactured in the United States of America

Website: http://greenhavenpublishing.com

Contents

Chapter 1: Should Space Exploration Be Privatized?

Chapter 2: Should We Seek Extraterrestrial Life?

The Importance of Opposing Viewpoints

Perhaps every generation experiences a period in time in which the populace seems especially polarized, starkly divided on the important issues of the day and gravitating toward the far ends of the political spectrum and away from a consensus-facilitating middle ground. The world that today's students are growing up in and that they will soon enter into as active and engaged citizens is deeply fragmented in just this way. Issues relating to terrorism, immigration, women's rights, minority rights, race relations, health care, taxation, wealth and poverty, the environment, policing, military intervention, the proper role of government—in some ways, perennial issues that are freshly and uniquely urgent and vital with each new generation—are currently roiling the world.

If we are to foster a knowledgeable, responsible, active, and engaged citizenry among today's youth, we must provide them with the intellectual, interpretive, and critical-thinking tools and experience necessary to make sense of the world around them and of the all-important debates and arguments that inform it. After all, the outcome of these debates will in large measure determine the future course, prospects, and outcomes of the world and its peoples, particularly its youth. If they are to become successful members of society and productive and informed citizens, students need to learn how to evaluate the strengths and weaknesses of someone else's arguments, how to sift fact from opinion and fallacy, and how to test the relative merits and validity of their own opinions against the known facts and the best possible available information. The landmark series Opposing Viewpoints has been providing students with just such critical-thinking skills and exposure to the debates surrounding society's most urgent contemporary issues for many years, and it continues to serve this essential role with undiminished commitment, care, and rigor.

The key to the series's success in achieving its goal of sharpening students' critical-thinking and analytic skills resides in its title—

Opposing Viewpoints. In every intriguing, compelling, and engaging volume of this series, readers are presented with the widest possible spectrum of distinct viewpoints, expert opinions, and informed argumentation and commentary, supplied by some of today's leading academics, thinkers, analysts, politicians, policy makers, economists, activists, change agents, and advocates. Every opinion and argument anthologized here is presented objectively and accorded respect. There is no editorializing in any introductory text or in the arrangement and order of the pieces. No piece is included as a "straw man," an easy ideological target for cheap point-scoring. As wide and inclusive a range of viewpoints as possible is offered, with no privileging of one particular political ideology or cultural perspective over another. It is left to each individual reader to evaluate the relative merits of each argument—as he or she sees it, and with the use of ever-growing critical-thinking skills—and grapple with his or her own assumptions, beliefs, and perspectives to determine how convincing or successful any given argument is and how the reader's own stance on the issue may be modified or altered in response to it.

This process is facilitated and supported by volume, chapter, and selection introductions that provide readers with the essential context they need to begin engaging with the spotlighted issues, with the debates surrounding them, and with their own perhaps shifting or nascent opinions on them. In addition, guided reading and discussion questions encourage readers to determine the authors' point of view and purpose, interrogate and analyze the various arguments and their rhetoric and structure, evaluate the arguments' strengths and weaknesses, test their claims against available facts and evidence, judge the validity of the reasoning, and bring into clearer, sharper focus the reader's own beliefs and conclusions and how they may differ from or align with those in the collection or those of their classmates.

Research has shown that reading comprehension skills improve dramatically when students are provided with compelling, intriguing, and relevant "discussable" texts. The subject matter of these collections could not be more compelling, intriguing, or urgently relevant to today's students and the world they are poised to inherit. The anthologized articles and the reading and discussion questions that are included with them also provide the basis for stimulating, lively, and passionate classroom debates. Students who are compelled to anticipate objections to their own argument and identify the flaws in those of an opponent read more carefully, think more critically, and steep themselves in relevant context, facts, and information more thoroughly. In short, using discussable text of the kind provided by every single volume in the Opposing Viewpoints series encourages close reading, facilitates reading comprehension, fosters research, strengthens critical thinking, and greatly enlivens and energizes classroom discussion and participation. The entire learning process is deepened, extended, and strengthened.

For all of these reasons, Opposing Viewpoints continues to be exactly the right resource at exactly the right time—when we most need to provide readers with the critical-thinking tools and skills that will not only serve them well in school but also in their careers and their daily lives as decision-making family members, community members, and citizens. This series encourages respectful engagement with and analysis of opposing viewpoints and fosters a resulting increase in the strength and rigor of one's own opinions and stances. As such, it helps make readers "future ready," and that readiness will pay rich dividends for the readers themselves, for the citizenry, for our society, and for the world at large.

Introduction

On October 4, 1957, the Soviet Union launched a satellite into space. It was called Sputnik 1 and was the first artificial satellite to orbit Earth. It was only about the size of a beachball and took just over an hour and a half to orbit the planet. Its impact, however, was huge and long-lasting. It is not an exaggeration to say that little Sputnik changed the world.

Today there are thousands of artificial satellites circling above us—built, launched, and operated by dozens of countries. These satellites monitor the weather, conduct scientific research, facilitate communications, and take care of many other tasks essential to modern life.

The decades after the launch of Sputnik were a golden age of space exploration and scientific research and innovation. The United States formed the National Aeronautics and Space Administration (NASA), an independent agency designed to "provide for research into problems of flight within and outside the earth's atmosphere." On July 20, 1969, US astronauts stepped out of their spacecraft and walked on the Moon. It was, as astronaut Neil Armstrong said, "One small step for man, one giant leap for mankind."

The Soviets continued their robust space program, and other nations got into the game as well. In recent years, funding for space research has been much harder to come by than it was in the 1960s and 1970s. However, space exploration has always been a passion, even when it was not a huge priority. Today, NASA is exploring Mars and planning a manned mission to the red planet. Roscosmos, Russia's space agency, is also sending missions to Mars, and is refining the techniques for staffing and supplying the International Space Station, exercises that will no doubt be very useful in future interplanetary expeditions. The International Space Station (an artificial satellite in which humans can live and work) has provided a base of operations for much groundbreaking research. It has also proved that researchers from many nations can work in harmony in the interests of all mankind.

However, in recent years, economic difficulties have led to reduced government funding for space research—especially as it relates to pure science and not military defense. As governments have pulled back the effort is being taken up by private investors. Tech entrepreneurs such as Elon Musk and Jeff Bezos have seen the chance for gaining even greater wealth by investing in space exploration. Space exploration started as a competition between superpower governments. Now it may be becoming a competition between superrich tech leaders.

Meanwhile, discoveries of large numbers of planets thought to be capable of sustaining life similar to life on Earth has reawakened the search for extraterrestrial life. A cadre of scientists is carefully watching the sky—and monitoring radio signals—for signs of intelligent life elsewhere in the universe. Philosophers as well as scientists are debating what to say and what to do if and when we finally make contact.

In the decades since the Cold War (1947–1991), space exploration and research has largely been undertaken for peaceful reasons. However, tensions between the world's spacefaring nations have been on the rise again, and nations relatively new to the space game, such as China, are adding to the unease. In 2018, US President Donald Trump recommended the creation of an additional branch of the US military—a space force. His remarks indicated that the purpose of the space force was not entirely peaceful. While many members of his own administration oppose the idea, it is not because they don't anticipate trouble in space.

All of the developments have raised many questions and generated fascinating debate, much of which is explored in *Opposing Viewpoints: The Future of Space Exploration*. In chapters titled "Should Space Exploration Be Privatized?" "Should We Seek Extraterrestrial Life?" "Is Space Exploration a Public Good?" and "Should We Militarize Space?" authors offer wide-ranging viewpoints that begin by examining the new role of entrepreneurs in space exploration, then go on to dissect issues ranging from the wisdom of calling out to potential extraterrestrials to the wisdom of militarizing space. The voices are intelligent, often passionate, and refreshingly lacking in acrimony, even when they are critical of other points of view.

Chapter 1

Should Space Exploration Be Privatized?

Chapter Preface

Space exploration has long been considered the purview of the government, primarily the governments of the United States and the former Soviet Union. The reasons for this are both practical and political. For most of our history, space exploration was too expensive and too risky for private companies to take on, while the profits were largely limited to long-term greater public good. And of course, the immediate goal of space innovation, whether in the United States or the Soviet Union, was to establish political dominance over that nation's enemies. Any public good that might accrue was a happy byproduct. Nowadays, government coffers are running low. Expensive projects like missions to Mars and exploration of outer space are hard to sell to taxpayers who can't afford basic needs like health insurance or higher education.

Business, on the other hand, is enjoying a gilded age. Private companies are finding that technological innovations and reduced production costs have made it feasible to take on the job of space exploration themselves. In fact, space may be awash in new business opportunities. The relatively mundane, such as launching and maintaining satellites and monitoring Earth's resources, are proving quite lucrative. Perhaps most tantalizingly, the mining of other heavenly bodies for resources that can be sold back on Earth promise private investors not only unimagined wealth but global influence and power as well. In today's climate of multibillion-dollar technology companies and individual tech tycoons looking for things to do with their boatloads of wealth, the glamour and excitement of space exploration is nigh irresistible.

The debate between capitalism and socialism is not likely to be resolved anytime soon, but when it comes to privatizing space exploration, issues go beyond the question of who should control the world's resources. In the following viewpoints, writers explore from an array of perspectives the question "Should Space Be Privatized?" They ask, "Are private companies both able and willing to make sure their rockets are safe? How will they deal with the inevitable moral questions that will arise when resources—or even other civilizations—are discovered? And most fundamentally, should we even be doing this in the first place, considering the fact that our own planet is in such dire need of care?" The viewpoints in this chapter are diverse, and often not at all what you might expect.

> *"I would hope that the main enabling factor in the pursuit of space endeavours is not possession of wealth, but that vision, ingenuity and a wish for the betterment of humans are the main driving forces."*

Private Enterprise Has Invigorated Space Exploration

Monica Grady

In the following viewpoint, Monica Grady argues that the space race still exists. It has just changed from being a competition for dominance between superpower nations to a competition for customers and profit between private businesses. Grady explains who these companies are and what they hope to accomplish. The major players, she points out, are all led by exceptionally passionate and charismatic leaders. This is leading to rapid progress. The question—and perhaps this greatest risk—according to Grady, is that the drive for wealth, rather than for innovation that will benefit all humankind, might not lead to the same good results as did the original space race. Grady is a leading British space scientist.

"Private Companies Are Launching A New Space Race – Here's What to Expect," by Monica Grady, The Conversation, October 3, 2017. https://theconversation.com/private-companies-are-launching-a-new-space-race-heres-what-to-expect-80697. Licensed Under CC BY-ND 4.0 International.

As you read, consider the following questions:

1. What, according to this viewpoint, are the main goals of the three major companies involved in space exploration?
2. Does this author think that privatization of space is resulting in faster innovation?
3. What particular risks does private exploration of space entail, according to Grady?

The space race between the USA and Russia started with a beep from the Sputnik satellite exactly 60 years ago (October 4, 1957) and ended with a handshake in space just 18 years later. The handshake was the start of many decades of international collaboration in space. But over the past decade there has been a huge change.

The space environment is no longer the sole preserve of government agencies. Private companies have entered the exploration domain and are propelling the sector forward more vigorously and swiftly than would be the case if left to governments alone.

It could be argued that a new space race has begun, in which private companies are competing against each other and against government organisations. But this time it is driven by a competition for customers rather than the urge to show dominance by being first to achieve a certain goal. So who are the main players and how will they change the science, technology and politics of space exploration?

Put the phrase "private space exploration" into a search engine and a wealth of links emerges. Several have titles such as: "Six private companies that could launch humans into space," "The world's top 10 most innovative companies in space" or "10 major players in the private sector space race." What is immediately apparent is that practically all these companies are based in the US.

There is a big difference between building and launching satellites into low Earth orbit for telecommunications and sending crew and cargo to the International Space Station (ISS) and beyond. Private companies in several nations have been engaged in the satellite market for many years. Their contributions to the development of non-governmental space exploration has helped to lay the trail for entrepreneurs with the vision and resources to develop their own pathways to space.

Today, several companies in the US are looking very specifically at human spaceflight. The three that are perhaps furthest down the road are SpaceX, Blue Origin and Virgin Galactic. The main goal of all three companies is to reduce the cost of access to space—mainly through reuse of launchers and spacecraft—making space accessible to people who are not specially trained astronauts. One thing these companies have in common is the private passion of their chief executives.

SpaceX was founded in 2002 by Elon Musk, a charismatic entrepreneur, engineer, inventor and investor. The ambition of SpaceX is "to revolutionise space technology, with the ultimate goal of enabling people to live on other planets." To this end, the company has specialised in the design, manufacture and launch of rockets, providing direct competition to the United Launch Alliance (between Boeing and Lockheed Martin) that had been the contract holder of choice for launch of NASA and Department of Defense rocket launches.

Its success has been spectacular. Having developed the Falcon 9 launch vehicle and Dragon spacecraft, it became the first commercial company to dock a spacecraft at the ISS in 2012. The firm now has a regular run there, carrying cargo. But so far, no astronauts. However, the Falcon Heavy is comparable to the Saturn 5 rocket that launched the Apollo astronauts, and SpaceX has designed its vehicle with a view to sending astronauts to the moon by 2018, and to Mars as early as 2023.

On September 29, Musk refined his plans, announcing the BFR project (which I like to pretend stands for Big F**king Rocket). This would replace the Falcon and Dragon spacecraft—and would not only transport cargo and explorers to the moon and Mars, but could also reduce travel times between cities on Earth. Musk calculates it could take as little as 29 minutes to fly from London to New York.

Whether the company succeeds in sending astronauts to the moon in 2018 remains to be seen. Either way, a lot could be going on then—2018 is also the year when Blue Origin, founded in 2000 by Jeff Bezos, the technology and retail entrepreneur behind Amazon, aims to launch people to space. But its ambition is different from that of SpaceX. Blue Origin is focusing on achieving commercially available, sub-orbital human spaceflight—targeting the space tourism industry. The company has developed a vertical launch vehicle (New Shepard, after the first American astronaut in space, Alan Shepard) that can reach the 100km altitude used to define where "space" begins. The rocket then descends back to Earth, with the engines firing towards the end of the descent, allowing the spacecraft to land vertically. Test flights with no passengers have made successful demonstrations of the technology. The trip to space and back will take about 10 minutes.

But Blue Origin has got some competition from Virgin Galactic, which describes itself as "the world's first commercial spaceline". Founded in 2004 by Richard Branson, also a technology and retail entrepreneur, it plans to carry six passengers at a time into sub-orbital space and give them about six minutes of weightlessness in the course of a two and a half hour flight.

The technology differs from that of SpaceX and Blue Origin in that the launch into space is not from the ground, but from a jet airplane. This mothership flies to an altitude of about 18km (about twice as high as regular aircraft fly) and releases a smaller, rocket-powered spacecraft (SpaceShip Two) which is propelled to an altitude of about 100km. The programme has been delayed by technical difficulties—and then by the tragic loss of pilot Mike Alsbury, when SpaceShip Two exploded in mid-air during a test flight in 2014. No date is yet set for the first passengers to fly.

There's also the Google Lunar XPrize competition, announced in 2007, with the tagline: "Welcome to the new space race". The aim of the prize is to launch a robotic mission to the moon, place a lander on the surface and drive 50 metres, sending back high-quality images and video. The competition is still in progress. Five privately funded teams must launch their spacecraft to the moon by the end of 2017.

Powerful International Ties

The changes are taking place against a backdrop of tried and tested international collaboration in space, which took off in earnest at the end of the space race. Throughout the 1980s and 1990s, the US and Russia space programmes complemented each other beautifully—though perhaps not intentionally. Following the cessation of Apollo in 1975, the US space programme focused its efforts on robotic exploration of the solar system.

The Voyager probes gave us amazing images of Jupiter, Saturn, Uranus and Neptune. The Mariner and Viking missions to Mars led to Pathfinder, Spirit, Opportunity and Curiosity. Messenger orbited Mercury and Magellan orbited Venus. When New Horizons launched to Pluto in 2006, it was a mission to visit the last planet left unexplored in the solar system.

Russia, on the other hand, pursued the goal of human spaceflight, with its incredibly successful Mir orbiting space station and its programme of flights to transfer cosmonauts and cargo backwards and forwards to Mir. Human spaceflight in the US revived with the Space Shuttle and its mission to build and occupy the International Space Station (ISS). The list of nations that contribute to the ISS continues to grow. The shuttle programme finished in 2011 and, since its successor Orion (built in collaboration with European Space Agency, ESA) is not due to come into service until at least 2023, the international community has been reliant on Russia to keep the ISS fuelled and inhabited.

Today, as well as the US and Russia, there are strong, vibrant and successful space programmes in Europe, Japan, India and China. The European Space Agency was established just two months before the historic handshake of 1975, following many years of independent aeronautical engineering research by individual nations. Similarly, the Chinese, Japanese and Indian space agencies can trace their heritages back to the 1960s. A number of smaller countries including the United Arab Emirates also have ambitious plans.

Of course these countries also compete against each other. There has been widespread speculation that the entry of China into the field was sufficient to introduce a fresh imperative to the US space programme. China has a well-developed space programme and is currently working towards having a space station in orbit around the Earth by about 2020. A prototype, Tiangong-2, has been in space for almost a year, and was occupied by two astronauts (or "taikonauts") for a month.

China has also had three successful missions to the moon. And its next mission, Chang'e 5, due to launch towards the end of 2017, is designed to bring samples from the moon back to Earth. China also has a declared intent of landing taikonauts on the moon by 2025—the same time frame in which the US will be testing its new Orion spacecraft in orbit around the moon.

But while there's an element of competition, the success of the past few decades certainly shows that it is possible to collaborate in space even when tensions rise on the ground. Indeed, space exploration may even act as a buffer zone from international politics, which is surely something worth having. It will be interesting to see how a wider role in space exploration for private companies will affect such international collaborations, especially since so much of the effort is based in the USA.

Healthy Competition or Dangerous Game?

A benefit of the entry of the private sector into space exploration has been recognition of the high-tech companies that contribute to the growth of the economy as valuable targets for investment. Indeed, a recent presentation at an international investment bank— under a heading of "Space; the next investment frontier"—declared that "investment interest has helped reduce launch costs and spur innovation across related industries, opening up a new chapter in the history of the space economy."

One of the last engagements of Barack Obama's presidency was to chair the Whitehouse Frontiers Conference, where space exploration was discussed as much within the context of US industry as within the drive to explore new worlds. Contributors to the conference included NASA—but overwhelmingly the speakers were from private technology and investment companies.

Perhaps it is cynical to say—but once investment starts to flow, lawyers won't be far behind. And that is another aspect of the explosion of interest in space commerce and tourism. Laws, statutes and other regulations are necessary to govern the international nature of space exploration. At the moment, the United Nations, through its Office for Outer Space Affairs, is responsible for promoting international cooperation in the peaceful uses of outer space. It also oversees operation of the Outer Space Treaty, which provides a framework for the governance of space and activities that might take place. While the obvious lack of "space police" means that it cannot be practically enforced, it has never actually been violated.

The operation is designed along similar lines to the international treaties that oversee maritime activities and the exploration of Antarctica. This is the closest that there is to international legislation and, since coming into operation in 1967 with the three inaugural signatories of the United States of America, the United Kingdom and the (then) USSR, the treaty has been signed by 106 countries (including China and North Korea). It is necessary to have such controls because although the risks that surround space exploration are high, potential rewards are even higher.

If we look at the way more conventional businesses operate, such as supermarkets, competition drives prices down, and there is little reason to believe that competition between space companies would follow a different model. In which case, greater risks might be taken in order to increase profitability. There is no evidence for this so far—but as the field develops and additional private companies move into space exploration—there will be a higher probability of accident or emergency.

The treaty says that a state launching a probe or satellite is liable to pay compensation for damage when accidents occur. However, the costs of space exploration are astronomical and crippling to poorer countries, making them increasingly depend on commercial launchers. But if a private company launches an object that subsequently causes damage in space, the struggling economy will have to pick up the bill. The treaty may therefore need to be updated to make private companies more liable. There are also serious issues around the safety of astronauts, who have the legal right to a safe existence when in outer space. But even lawyers aren't sure whether the law does—or should—extend to private astronauts.

Looking to the future, there will be a need for an expanded version of a Civil Aviation Authority, directing and controlling routes, launches and landings on Earth, and between and on planetary bodies. All the safety and security considerations of air and sea travel will pertain to space travel at a vastly enhanced level, because the costs and risks are so much higher. There will have to be firm and well-understood protocols in the event of a spacecraft crashing, or two spacecraft colliding. Not to mention piracy or the possibility of hijack. All this might sound a little gloomy, taking the dash and exhilaration from space exploration, but it will be a necessary development that opens up the era of space travel for citizens beyond those with deep pockets.

The original space race resulted from the ideas and skills of visionary theoretician engineers including: Robert H Goddard, Wernher von Braun, Konstantin E. Tsiolkovsky... Is it too far a stretch to think that the second space race is propelled by a new generation of entrepreneurs, including Bezos, Branson and Musk? If this is the situation, then I would hope that the main enabling factor in the pursuit of space endeavours is not possession of wealth, but that vision, ingenuity and a wish for the betterment of human are the main driving forces.

"Humans will have new questions to ponder as we return to the moon, dig beneath Mars' surface, and peek around the far side of Pluto. And many of these questions have roots on Earth."

Private Space Exploration Raises Political and Moral Issues

Leigh Cooper

While many are excited about the possibilities of privately funded space exploration, it raises a lot of questions. In the following viewpoint Leigh Cooper explores what we can expect from the future of this model. Private enterprises can provide far more funding than NASA could hope to, and the possibilities for new resources are exciting. However, as the astronomer quoted in this piece points out, that will bring all sorts of new issues and decisions—including, perhaps, many vexing moral questions. We can travel to space, but we cannot get away from ourselves, and our controversies. Cooper is a science writer based in Santa Cruz, California.

"Space Privatization, Tourism and Morals," by Leigh Cooper, American Institute of Physics, March 24, 2015. Reprinted by permission.

As you read, consider the following questions:

1. Why, according to this viewpoint, is NASA no longer able to be as innovative as it was in the 1960s?
2. What non-financial costs of space exploration does this viewpoint address?
3. How, according to the people quoted in this viewpoint, might space exploration lead to war and genocide?

N ovel technologies, innovative engineering and breathtaking discoveries could be the story of the next 100 years of space exploration. But space travel involves more than math, telescopes and rovers according to the speakers at a session at last month's annual meeting of the American Association for the Advancement of Science in San Jose, California. Modern space exploration mixes together governments and private companies, science and ethics, promise and possibilities.

Chris Impey, an astronomer at the University of Arizona in Tucson, thinks that the desire to explore, which has pushed humans to cross oceans and conquer mountains, will continue to propel humans into space.

"I think what is happening now is as profound as the transition that took place among hunter gatherers when they left Africa 50 or 60 thousand years ago," said Impey. "It took an amazing short time—just a couple hundred generations—for simple tribal units of 50 or 100 to spread essentially across the Earth."

And space exploration is about to pick up, according to Impey. The original 1960s space race that spawned the Apollo missions rose out of geopolitical strife during the Cold War. Now, the federal funds for space travel are drying up. In the mid-1960s the NASA budget topped out at almost 4.5 percent of the US Government's budget, a number that has now shrunk to roughly 0.5 percent.

"NASA has very little slack in its budget for new, clever initiatives," said Impey. "We are now witnessing a transition to a more private enterprise driven space program."

IS THE TIME FOR SPACE EXPLORATION OVER?

The shuttle Atlantis has left the international space station and is headed for its last landing at the Kennedy Space Centre in Florida. As the shuttle undocked, astronaut Chris Ferguson said: "As the ISS now enters the era of utilisation, we'll never forget the role played by the space shuttle in its creation. Like a proud parent, we anticipate great things to follow from the men and women who build, operate and live there."

The retirement of the shuttle mission leaves a gap in the space programme. The ultimate dream of a manned mission to Mars seems as distant as ever, and in this time of recession the expense of space travel seems hard to justify to the public.

Is it time to accept that we have gone as far as we can with space exploration? Or should mankind remember the words of HG Wells—"Life, for ever dying to be born afresh, for ever young and eager, will presently stand upon this earth as upon a footstool, and stretch out its realm amidst the stars"—and continue to explore the final frontier? And if so, why?

"Should We End Space Exploration?" Guardian News and Media Limited, July 19, 2011.

He thinks the rise of space travel will mirror the development of the Internet. Impey explained, that people have forgotten many of the first Internet pioneers—those who came even before the military began investing in the Internet. Since then, the Internet has expanded with the commercial sector driving much of the innovation.

Over the next 100 years, we could decide to tackle anything from building a space elevator on the moon to sending nanobot probes to another star system or even constructing a space colony, said Impey.

"We don't know who the Googles and the Amazons are going to be. It might be SpaceX and Virgin Galactic," Impey said about the private groups who will be involved in the next stage in space travel. "I do believe that what happens next [with space travel] will dwarf what's happened before."

But progress will not come without cost. Impey reminded the audience that these continued forays into space will likely include accidents like those that occurred in October 2014: the Orbital rocket explosion and the Virgin Galactic SpaceShipTwo crash, which killed one pilot and injured another.

"People died in the first decade of the civil aviation program," said Impey. "There are going to be ups and downs."

Tourism also will play a role in moving space exploration forward. For example, Guy Laliberté, the founder of Cirque du Soleil, paid $20 million for a 9-day visit to the International Space Station and an additional $15 million for a spacewalk. Now, singer Sarah Brightman has announced she will soon travel to space; she will sing a new song by ex-husband Sir Andrew Lloyd Webber on the International Space Station. Enviable vacations, but not your average travel agent bill.

Currently it costs $3,000-4,000 per kilogram to send a payload to space, but Impey says that cost can easily come down to a few hundred dollars per kilogram by applying clever engineering to modern technology, opening the door for increased tourism.

And there's money lurking beyond those moons. Asteroids and comets could be mined or foreign bacteria or viruses—if found—could be used in pharmaceutical development. The competition could become fierce for rights to own space.

"We have a fraught history of figuring out who owns what," said Sara Waller, a philosopher at Montana State University in Bozeman. Ownership questions that plague us on Earth will rear up as we move off planet, she warns.

The premise of ownership has resulted in conflict and compromise throughout human history, pointed out Waller. In the US, settlers' claims for space overlapped with those of Native Americans. Aggression and genocide erupted as so many people vied for the rich resources.

On the other hand, countries have parceled off Antarctica without heady conflicts.

"This has nice analogies for what we are doing in space," said Waller. "It's a great big place. Not a whole lot of people yet needing to go out there. So far so good."

Finding unbiased mediators to settle overlapping country claims in space will be difficult, Waller anticipates.

Humans will have new questions to ponder as we return to the moon, dig beneath Mars' surface, and peek around the far side of Pluto. And many of these questions have roots on Earth. The US and other countries have and will continue to debate how to treat wild and historic places, weighting protection and development.

Outside our atmosphere, we will tackle these questions again when we ponder whether to treat the Apollo landing sites as historic landmarks and not disturb the footprints. If we find Martian microbes, does Mars belong to them or to us? Can or should we develop it? And what happens if we come across something bigger among the stars?

"What if they were tiger-like, frog-like, or human-like?" asked Waller. "Do human needs come first?"

> *"[T]he Moon should be treated no differently from international waters —nobody has to own the waters to be able to use the resources."*

International Law Will Refine Ownership Questions and Mining Rights for Private Space Exploration Companies

Nadine Cranenburgh

Space companies are designing innovative rockets and are well on their way to being able to mine the Moon, and eventually stake out claims on other space bodies as well. The previous viewpoint explored some of the challenges and potential controversies this might pose. In the following viewpoint Nadine Cranenburgh quotes a source who suggests a possible answer to at least one of these dilemmas. When it comes to ownership, space bodies, such as the Moon, should be treated just like international waters. Cranenburgh is an electrical engineer and journalist in Australia.

"Why Private Industry Is the Next Wave of Space Exploration," by Nadine Cranenburgh, Create Digital, January 29, 2018. Reproduced with permission from Engineers Australia's CREATE magazine. All rights reserved. https://www.createdigital.org.au/private-industry-space-exploration/.

As you read, consider the following questions:

1. Why do you think monitoring is a focus of Rocket Lab's mission?
2. Space exploration is described here as an emerging "market." Do you find that encouraging or disturbing? Why?
3. Can you think of scenarios in which treating rights the Moon and other space bodies like international waters might not work?

Once considered the realm of governments and superpowers, entrepreneurs are leading the new space race. Now, private companies are pushing the boundaries of space exploration and could even seek mining rights for the Moon as early as this year.

Footage from the recent launch of Rocket Lab's Electron vehicle and kick stage separation was streamed live on social media from its launch pad in Mahia, New Zealand, prompting excitement in the international space industry.

The rocket, with the unassuming name of "Still Testing," released four satellites for commercial customers. These included two Spire Global Lemur-2 satellites, which will join a constellation that tracks and monitors shipping and weather patterns on Earth. The third satellite was a Planet Dove satellite that will provide images of Earth's surface. (The fourth satellite was a secret payload, later revealed to be The Humanity Star, a geodesic carbon fibre sphere with 65 reflective panels to create a bright flashing effect in the sky.)

According to Rocket Lab CEO Peter Beck, monitoring is a key focus of this mission.

"This is not just about getting to orbit. We're really looking to get all the data we can," Beck told CNBC.

This is the first test for the rocket's deployment systems, which Beck said is a crucial step in supporting their plans for an increased market share.

"It's not like we're looking to build one or two vehicles this year. We're really looking to kick it into an unprecedented flight rate," Beck said.

The Electron rockets have a price tag of $5 million each, which might be economical enough to allow Rocket Lab to meet their ambitions for a high launch volume.

This success follows a near miss in December last year, where the company's maiden launch failed to reach orbit due to an automatic shutdown.

Fit for Purpose

Rocket Lab's design aesthetic highlights one of the potential trends of this new wave of space exploration. Startups keen to maximise use and profit can create more multi-use vessels, with features that cater to a variety of needs.

For example, the Electron rocket has a "plug-in payload" system, which decouples payload integration from the rest of the design. It also has a kick stage that can execute multiple burns, meaning different payloads can be placed in different orbits.

Carbon composite materials, and custom cryogenic valves and helium pressurised systems, create a strong yet lightweight structure to provide weight savings and insure delivery as much as possible.

Even the hardware and avionics can be customised.

"The computing nodes make use of state-of-the-art FPGA architecture, allowing massive customisation of function while retaining hardware commonality," according to Rocket Lab's website.

Mines and Men on the Moon

Following its successful launch, Rocket Lab is in a good position to supply the five rockets it is due to provide this year to aspiring lunar mining firm Moon Express.

Moon Express has announced its ambitions to tap into the commercial possibilities of lunar resources such as precious minerals, water and iron ore. Moon Express Chairman Naveen

Jain expressed confidence in pulling off the first private moon landing in 2018.

He said that a private lunar mission will put entrepreneurs on par with the world's superpowers.

"And imagine the entrepreneurs doing things that only the three superpowers have done before," Jain mused.

Jain's plans don't end there. By 2022, he plans to make the moon the "eighth continent."

"We are going to have a permanent presence there, we are going to have internet there and we are going to be able to communicate just like we communicate from here to even Australia," Jain told CNBC.

Moon Express is one of four finalists in Google's $20 million USD Lunar Xprize competition, which has encouraged a push for private space exploration over the past decade.

Google has recently announced that it does not intend to extend the Xprize competition past its current 31 March deadline, although it is unlikely that any of the finalists will make a lunar touchdown by this date.

At time of writing, Google had not provided a reason for this decision, although they have granted two previous time extensions: first to 2012, then to this year.

Who Owns Space?

The private sector's space invasion prompts questions about the ownership of the final frontier.

According to an agreement made by the US and Russia during the first space race, no country is able to claim sovereignty over the realms outside Earth's atmosphere.

But what about companies seeking to profit from extraterrestrial resources?

After gaining permission for their first moon mission from the US Government, Jain claims that the laws around private space exploration will be clarified as entrepreneurs continue to push the envelope.

"First of all, the Moon should be treated no differently from international waters—nobody has to own the waters to be able to use the resources," Jain said.

The Australian Government is keen for local companies to claim their slice of the emerging multi-billion dollar international space industry, and are due to release a review of our homegrown prospects in March, so watch this space (pun intended).

> *"It's outrageous that there are billions of dollars available for space missions, but never enough to properly fund education and healthcare. And of course it's crazy that the world has managed to provide space tourism before it's provided clean water for all the world's population."*

If We Can Send a Car into Space, We Can Stop Climate Change

Jeremy Williams

In the following viewpoint, Jeremy Williams raises a very different kind of question about the morality of space exploration. How, he asks, can we justify the exorbitant cost of space exploration when there are so many problems we still need to solve on our own planet—not the least of which is making sure it remains habitable. Williams argues that investment in space exploration could lead to more economic opportunity and therefore greater resources for addressing these problems. And the innovative thinking required by the enterprise could stimulate solutions to other problems as well. Williams is a writer and community activist in England.

"What to Make of SpaceX in an Age of Inequality?" by Jeremy Williams, Make Wealth History, February 7, 2018. Reprinted by permission.

As you read, consider the following questions:

1. The viewpoint author argues that ending poverty and going to Mars aren't mutually exclusive. If there is enough money to end poverty, why hasn't it been done?
2. How, according to the author, does wealth inequality make it more difficult to solve social problems?
3. Do you agree with the author's optimism that in a world in which a man can send his car into space, we can certainly solve poverty and stop climate change?

Last night after dinner I was talking to my kids about SpaceX and the test of the Falcon Heavy rocket, which will one day carry people to Mars. I was hoping to watch the launch live with them, but it was pushed back past their bedtimes by the weather in Florida. I showed them the animation of Elon Musk's Tesla roadster being launched into orbit instead.

My wife's reaction was to simply ask "why are you so excited about this?" and that's a response I've heard a few times when I express my enthusiasm for space. The implication is that as someone who cares about poverty, inequality and the environment, I should consider the very idea of space travel to be a massive and expensive distraction.

I get where those comments come from. Of course it's frustrating that we can commit to twenty-year plans to put probes on distant planets, but can't commit to looking after the only planet we've actually got. It's outrageous that there are billions of dollars available for space missions, but never enough to properly fund education and healthcare. And of course it's crazy that the world has managed to provide space tourism before it's provided clean water for all the world's population.

I get all of that. Does that mean SpaceX shouldn't exist? No.

For a start, it isn't as if there is a big global pot of money sitting there for humanity to allocate on an either/or basis—Mars mission or toilets? Even Elon Musk doesn't have a big pot of money to

AMERICANS SUPPORT SPACE EXPLORATION—BUT AREN'T SO SURE ABOUT PAYING FOR IT

Americans are supportive of the space program and space exploration. In a 2011 Pew Research survey, 58% of Americans said it is essential that the US be a world leader in space exploration.

Some 38% said they think the space program contributes "a lot" to scientific advancements that Americans can use, and another 36% said the program contributes "some" to such advancements. Most also said that the space program contributes a lot (34%) or some (34%) to America's national pride and patriotism.

Americans were also supportive of specific aspects of the US space program, such as the space shuttle program and the International Space Station. About two-thirds (64%) of the public said the space station has been a good investment for the country, while 29% said it was not a good investment, according to our 2014 survey. And the 2011 poll found that 55% of Americans said that the space shuttle program had been a good investment for the country, compared with 36% who said it was not a good investment.

In a January 2015 survey, 68% of Americans expressed a favorable view of NASA, similar to that of the Centers for Disease

allocate that way. Most of his wealth is on paper and he still has to raise funds for his ventures. Huge business projects like SpaceX generate the funding that they need in all sorts of ways that are closed to other causes, however worthwhile they may be. Maybe in an ideal world it would, but in this one stopping SpaceX would not free up money for more important things.

It's also worth remembering that money can be understood as a flow as well as a stock. When I bought my house, the asking price I paid was not somehow locked into the walls. The previous owner got a bank transfer for that amount, and then maybe went and bought a car. And the person who sold their car celebrated by going to Nandos, and the money flows out into the economy. In the same way, if SpaceX spends a billion dollars on a project,

Control and Prevention among the eight federal agencies we asked about. (Seven-in-ten had a favorable view of the CDC.) This was in line with similar favorable ratings for NASA in the past.

Americans are optimistic about the future of space exploration. A 2010 survey conducted by Pew Research and Smithsonian magazine found that 63% of Americans expected astronauts to land on Mars, and 53% believed that ordinary people would be able to travel in space by 2050. Some Americans are even more hopeful about the possibilities of space exploration. One-third of Americans predicted in a 2014 Pew Research/Smithsonian survey that humans will have long-term space colonies in the next 50 years.

Although they value the program and are proud of its achievements, Americans are reluctant to pay more for space exploration. Just 23% of Americans said the US spends too little on space exploration, according the National Opinion Research Center's General Social Survey (GSS) conducted last year. About four-in-ten (42%) said the US spends about the right amount, and 25% said the US spends too much on space exploration. Americans were more likely to say the government is spending too little on areas such as education (70%) and health (57%).

"5 Facts About Americans' Views on Space Exploration," by Brian Kennedy, Pew Research Center, July 14, 2015.

that money is not lost or destroyed, despite the image of it being blasted into space. Where did the billion go? Out into the bank accounts of SpaceX employees and suppliers, and then out again to wherever they go shopping, or pay their rent, and so on. The billion still exists. It's just not all in one place anymore, if it ever was. And it's already being spent again.

In other words, ending poverty and going to Mars aren't mutually exclusive. There should be money enough for both.

That doesn't mean we can ignore how money is spent entirely. There is such a thing as opportunity cost, and waste or negative consequences. In some situations, including a lot of government budgeting, there are either/or decisions being made. But when we see eye-watering sums of money being spent—whether it's on rockets or sports or paintings—asking "why wasn't that money spent on the poor" isn't a question that gets us very far. It's more important to ask, if there is so much money available, why isn't it flowing to where it's most needed?

This, incidentally, is one of the many problems with inequality. It stops the flow. When too much wealth accrues to a few people at the top, they can end up with more money than they could possibly spend or give away in a lifetime. It ends up hoarded away, out of circulation. Hoarded wealth ceases to serve any useful function other than to continue bloating in a tax haven somewhere.

To return to space, even if we can square away the expense, we might still conclude that space exploration is a waste of time and attention. But we could say that about all exploration. Christopher Columbus's mum probably wanted him to stay at home. Dissenting voices at the admiralty no doubt grumbled at the cost of the Beagle voyages. If you don't go, you'll never know what you might have found. Future generations will be the judge of whether our own exploration was worthwhile or not.

Personally, I'm excited that my children are growing up in a new space age. I like that this one is less nationalistic, and that prices are falling to the point that more countries are able to participate. Access to space is being democratized, and could play more of a role in poverty and development than we might assume. I like the way SpaceX and their rivals Blue Origin have pioneered re-useable boosters, and that because business is now taking the lead, there is a concern for using resources well that wasn't there when space was government funded.

Perhaps most of all, big projects inspire big projects. Whether you like Elon Musk or not, you can't help but admire his ambitions and his companies' ability to get stuff done. Last night a man successfully sent his car into space. Over breakfast I showed my kids the live video feed from the car, as the earth rotated into view. In such a world, we can do anything—including stopping climate change, and ending poverty.

| "*Spacex, among Musk's other companies, is only competitive and inexpensive because of government subsidies.*"

Private Space Companies Aren't as Private as You Think

Mitchell Gunter

The previous articles have assumed—or at least given the impression— that private space exploration is being done with private funding. In the following viewpoint Mitchell Gunter reports that these companies are heavily dependent on taxpayer support, either through public- private partnerships, government contracts, or subsidies. According to this reporting, SpaceX has received billions of dollars in government subsidies. That raises the question of just how private is private space exploration. Gunter is a conservative journalist who advocates for constitutional liberty, free speech, and the marketplace of ideas.

"SpaceX Wants to Fuel Deep Space Exploration with Your Money," by Mitchell Gunter, Foundation for Economic Education, September 4, 2017. https://fee.org/articles/spacex -wants-to-fuel-deep-space-exploration-with-your-money. Licensed Under CC BY 4.0 International.

As you read, consider the following questions:

1. What, according to this viewpoint, are the advantages of government and private enterprise working together on space projects?
2. How does the author suggest that the system for awarding government contracts might not work so well in the case of space exploration companies?
3. Do you agree with the author that American taxpayers are being "robbed" by private companies that take government dollars to develop their businesses? Why or why not?

In the aftermath of President Obama's cuts to NASA, and due to the agency's subsequent reliance on Russia, NASA has invested billions of dollars into private space companies to carry cargo and, eventually, astronauts to the International Space Station. NASA's private contracts have offered a "fixed price" for commercial services and required companies to provide their own funding to develop new spacecraft and rockets.

SpaceX, a private space company founded by Canadian-American business magnate Elon Musk, is one such contractor. Recently, SpaceX along with companies such as Blue Origin and Orbital ATK have raised eyebrows with plans to develop large, heavy-lift rockets, which will allow travel beyond low-Earth orbit.

One of these systems is SpaceX's Falcon Heavy booster, a rocket possessing 90 percent of the lift capability to low Earth orbit of NASA's own Space Launch System. The message is clear—these companies wish to attempt what NASA has not yet achieved.

Out of Orbit

Thus far, NASA's funding of private space companies has been limited to near-Earth endeavors—and NASA wants to keep it that way. Charles Bolden, NASA's 2016 administrator, expressed that deep space is traditionally NASA's domain during a Q&A session.

"If you talk about launch vehicles, we believe our responsibility to the nation is to take care of things that normal people cannot do, or don't want to do, like large launch vehicles," Bolden stated, concluding, "I'm not a big fan of commercial investment in large launch vehicles just yet."

However, some companies aren't content to leave deep space to NASA, but they still want the US taxpayer to foot the bill. During a hearing before the US Senate's Subcommittee on Space, Science, and Competitiveness on July 20th, SpaceX called upon the government to financially support deep space public-private partnerships.

Tim Hughes, SpaceX's senior Vice-President for Global Business and Government Affairs, testified, "The principles applied in past programs for low Earth orbit capability can, and should, be applied to deep space exploration," referring to NASA's Commercial Orbital Transportation Services (COTS) program.

Floating the idea of funding a COTS-like program, Hughes expressed his desire to work "in parallel" with NASA's Space Launch System and Orion spacecraft to facilitate deep space exploration. Nevertheless, Hughes acknowledged that the realm of deep space exploration is traditionally NASA's territory, stating, "There's a program of record right now that is NASA's central focus for deep space exploration."

While this is a nice idea in theory, companies with a track record like SpaceX's shouldn't be given contracts for deep space exploration, especially when tax dollars are at risk.

Cheaper Isn't Necessarily Better

SpaceX's Falcon 9 rocket exploded on the launch-pad on September 1, 2016. Likewise, on June 28, 2015, another Falcon 9 rocket exploded over the Atlantic Ocean, totaling $112 million in losses. These losses included reserves of food, water, and oxygen for the International Space Station, and two docking adapters for commercial crew vehicles.

Trusting resupply missions to private companies in near-Earth orbit is one thing. Trusting human lives to private companies in deep, unexplored space is quite another. All factors need to be considered for a project, not simply the base price—especially reliability.

Detailed and realistic planning is another factor that needs to be addressed. SpaceX's Interplanetary Transport System (ITS), a massive craft designed to take people to Mars, has faced tremendous design challenges. Nevertheless, Musk has outlined an ambitious plan to colonize Mars with approximately one million people.

Wisely, citing basic economic concerns, Musk suggested via Twitter that he would be scaling back the massive 12 meter ITS plans, stating, "A 9m diameter vehicle fits in our existing factories…"

Currently, the government is required to award contracts to private companies via a bidding process called, "Lowest Price Technology Acceptable." While the merits of this process are clear —namely protecting taxpayers from fraud and abuse—the system does present notable dangers.

Typically, the contract is awarded to the lowest bid with a "technically acceptable" proposal. Although this certainly factors in cost, it doesn't always factor in durability, quality, or reliability. Excluding these factors often results in companies lowballing their bids, and delivering poor-quality products.

Private, Not "Private"

Despite massive failures, SpaceX's argument is that it should continue to receive government contracts simply because it is the least expensive option. Companies like SpaceX may often be the cheapest solution, but the government should look beyond the base price tag when the risks are so high.

SpaceX, among Musk's other companies, is only competitive and inexpensive because of government subsidies. That is why Musk's condemnation of government subsidies is the height of irony. Musk's businesses have received a staggering $4.9 billion in government subsidies.

The space industry is the future, but that future doesn't have to come at the expense of free market principles. In order to earn the moniker "private," space companies must remain so, prudently refraining from robbing the American taxpayer in order to develop rockets capable of deep space exploration.

Periodical and Internet Sources Bibliography

The following articles have been selected to supplement the diverse views presented in this chapter.

Emily Baumgaertner, "Space Station Could Be Split to Aid Privatization, New NASA Chief Says," *New York Times*, June 6, 2018. https://www .nytimes.com/2018/06/06/science/space-station-nasa-bridenstine.html.

Denise Chow, "Commercial Space Travel May Bring Science Benefits, Advocates Say," Space.com, June 20, 2012. https://www.space .com/16228-nasa-commercial-human-spaceflight-benefits.html.

Alex Eichler, "The Pros and Cons of Privatized Space Exploration," *Atlantic*, February 15, 2010. https://www.theatlantic.com /technology/archive/2010/02/the-pros-and-cons-of-privatized-space -exploration/346657.

Loren Grush, "Private Space Companies Avoid FAA Oversight Again, with Congress' Blessing," *The Verge*, November 16, 2015. https://www. theverge.com/2015/11/16/9744298/private-space-government -regulation-spacex-asteroid-mining.

Kristin Houser, "Private Companies, Not Governments, Are Shaping the Future of Space Exploration," Futurism, June 12, 2017. https://futurism .com/private-companies-not-governments-are-shaping-the-future-of -space-exploration.

Konstantin Kakaes, "NASA's Leader Wants to Privatize the International Space Station. It's a Remarkably Terrible Idea," *Vox*, June 9, 2018. https:// www.vox.com/the-big-idea/2018/6/8/17438332/privatizing -international-space-station-iss-nasa-bridenstine.

Jason Koebler, "Meet the Truthers Who Are Certain SpaceX Faked Its Rocket Landing," *Motherboard*, April 13, 2016. https://motherboard .vice.com/en_us/article/nz7e4z/meet-the-truthers-who-believe-spacex -faked-its-rocket-landing.

Andy Meek, "Neil deGrasse Tyson: Don't Leave Space Exploration up to Private Companies," *BGR*, December 3, 2015. https://bgr .com/2015/12/03/neil-degrasse-tyson-interview-space-exploration.

Sanjana Varghese, "One Small Step for Private Companies: How the Future of Space Travel Is Being Redefined, *New Statesman America*, 9 January 2018. https://www.newstatesman.com/science-tech/space/2018/01/one-small -step-private-companies-how-future-space-travel-being-redefined.

Mark R. Whittington, "SpaceX Is Not a Threat to NASA," *The Hill*, June 10, 2018. https://thehill.com/opinion/technology/391532-spacex-is-not-a -threat-to-nasa.

CHAPTER 2

Should We Seek Extraterrestrial Life?

Chapter Preface

Searching outer space for resources is one thing. But searching it for other intelligent life forms is quite another. In the last chapter, a variety of authors expressed views about space exploration's potential to bring about wars, colonization, and debates over the ownership of resources that might be found among the stars as private companies seek profit there. In this chapter, authors offer viewpoints about the possibility that space is teeming with intelligent life—and whether or not it is wise to attempt to contact with that life.

Physicist Enrico Fermi proposed what has come to be known as the Fermi paradox: There are billions of stars similar to our sun. There has been plenty of time for at least some of them to develop intelligent life and technological civilizations similar to our own. So why haven't we heard from them? The viewpoints here tackle that paradox from a variety of perspectives. Some state reasons for believing that it is highly unlikely that we will ever encounter other beings enough like ourselves that we could communicate with them. Others think that the event is unavoidable, that we've already made a sort of contact (via our radio signals) and are merely waiting to see who responds and how they do so.

However the key question brought up by all these viewpoints is whether or not we should try to make contact with as yet unknown alien lifeforms. Several writers here mention Stephen Hawking's famous comment: "If aliens visit us, the outcome would be much as when Columbus landed in America, which didn't turn out well for the Native Americans." And in these viewpoints you will find a wide range of responses to Hawking's warning.

While reading this chapter, it is important to keep in mind the difference between extraterrestrial life and extraterrestrial intelligence. Finding microbes or rudimentary life forms could certainly pose some risks, but those are not precisely the risks that Hawking was talking about. Here, the viewpoints are concerned with intelligent life, the kind that could intentionally make contact and, perhaps, intentionally harm us.

> *"[T]he riskier, more audacious hunts for life elsewhere are driven by private money, not governments and national space agencies."*

Private Companies Are Better Able to Take Risks to Find Extraterrestrial Life

Ian Sample

In 2017, Earth had a tantalizing visitor. This was the first known interstellar object to pass through our solar system. Certain characteristics of the object indicated the possibility that it might have been the work of an alien civilization. Tests suggested otherwise, however. In the following viewpoint Ian Sample argues that while UFO sightings are generally not credible, the scientific search for extraterrestrial life most certainly is. Science strongly suggests that life is very likely to exist on other places besides Earth. The question that remains is who should conduct the search. Sample is a science correspondent for The Guardian.

"Why We Keep Scanning the Skies for Signs of Alien Intelligence," by Ian Sample, Guardian News and Media Limited, December 22, 2017. Reprinted by permission.

As you read, consider the following questions:

1. The author quotes Andrew Siemion as saying that extraterrestrials have likely not ever visited our solar system. How does he back up this claim?
2. Why, according to this viewpoint, are government agencies increasingly leaving the UFO hunting to private companies?
3. Where do the scientists quoted in this article think is the most likely place to find alien life?

I n less than an hour, the decision was made. It was 2 December and Avi Loeb, an astronomy professor at Harvard, was with Yuri Milner, the Russian billionaire and founder of Breakthrough Listen, a $100m alien-hunting venture. Milner had invited Loeb, an adviser on the project, to his Palo Alto home to discuss the bizarre features of the interstellar object, 'Oumuamua.

The first known visitor from another solar system, the monolithic lump appeared long and slender, a curious shape for a space rock. The two agreed there was the slimmest chance 'Oumuamua was not what it seemed. Eleven days later, Breakthrough Listen swung the world's largest steerable telescope, at Green Bank in West Virginia, into position and scanned the 400-metre-long body for signs that it was a passing spacecraft.

It was a long shot. After 10 hours of observations the telescope, which can detect a mobile phone signal at twice the distance of the sun, found no evidence that 'Oumuamua was the work of an alien civilisation. By all accounts, it is a dark, skyscraper-sized lump of carbon, ice and dust that simply tumbled into our solar system from, well, somewhere beyond. But even as the search came up empty, it proved a point: the riskier, more audacious hunts for life elsewhere are driven by private money, not governments and national space agencies.

It is not the only example. Earlier this week, the US Department of Defense confirmed that from 2007 it ran a programme to investigate unidentified flying object (UFO) sightings, but dropped funding five years later in favour of more pressing concerns. Luis Elizondo, the military intelligence official who ran the Advanced Aerospace Threat Identification Program, as the effort was named, resigned in October. He has since joined a private venture to continue his work in the field.

Of all the methods brought to bear on the question of life elsewhere, UFO sightings are at the farthest end of the credibility scale. When Monica Grady oversaw Britain's meteorite collection at the Natural History Museum in London, she received plenty of letters about alien spacecraft over Britain. Most ended up in the bin, but one exemplified the problem many scientists have with such reports. It came from a man who had photographed what he described as an alien vessel at the bottom of his garden. No one else noticed it, he noted ruefully, but he was adamant the spacecraft was responsible for road rage, cot death and measles. "For me, it's the difference between astrology and astronomy," said Grady, now professor of planetary science at the Open University. "We don't have any credible sightings that are more likely to be an alien spacecraft than not."

Few scientists would bet on finding anything more exotic than extraterrestrial microbes, in our solar system at least. "We are not expecting to get to the bottom of Enceladus's ocean and find a whole load of gnomes smelting metal," said Grady, referring to the tantalising subterranean water on the moon of Saturn, which occasionally sends geysers into space.

Andrew Siemion, who leads the Breakthrough Listen effort at the Berkeley Search for Extraterrestrial Intelligence Research Center in California, is sceptical that UFOs have ever visited Earth. "Astronomers of all types spend their lives looking up at the sky with every conceivable instrument we can build, and we do so independently, and we have never taken a picture of a spaceship.

And I can tell you every single graduate student and postdoc would love nothing more than to be the one to take that photo."

No wonder, then, that governments leave the more speculative searches for alien life to others. The programmes they do fund tend to avoid all mention of UFOs – the term has lost its intentional ambiguity since it was coined in the 1950s and become synonymous with alien spacecraft. Instead, programmes emphasise the potential threats posed by unexplained aerial objects that might be the secretive work of hostile nations. When Nick Pope worked on UFO sightings at the UK Ministry of Defence in the 1990s, all mention of UFOs was scrubbed in favour of the more fundable UAP, or Unidentified Aerial Phenomena. "The term UFO has a lot of pop culture baggage," Pope told the *Guardian*. "It will never really lose its fringe tag."

While ufology struggles for credibility, the search for alien transmissions is serious science. Much of the sky has been swept for alien signals in the form of optical, infrared and radio waves. But the searches are far from extensive. Future scans could tune into directed energy beams used to propel craft, x-ray and gamma-ray broadcasts, or even gravitational radiation. When the massive radio telescope known as the Square Kilometre Array comes online in 2020 or thereabouts, it will be the first facility that is sensitive enough to detect the equivalent of TV broadcasts on planets around Alpha Centauri, the closest star system to Earth. Pope believes that it is searches like these that will finally answer the question "are we alone?"

Discoveries from land and space telescopes, and robotic planetary missions, strongly suggest that life should exist elsewhere. Water and organic molecules needed for life as we know it are ubiquitous in space. And from NASA's Kepler mission, astronomers now believe that almost every star in the galaxy has at least one orbiting planet. "Everything necessary for life to arise and thrive on this planet exists in abundance throughout the universe," said Siemion.

The question, then, is where has life gained a foothold? "It should be on Europa, a moon of Jupiter; it should be at the bottom of Enceladus's ocean, and it should be on Mars," said Grady. "If the processes that got life going on Earth are universal, then some form of life should have got going."

"The reason people are so incredibly interested and excited is that it's such a profound human question. We have a basic desire to know what is beyond, what is out there," said Siemion. "What we have done so far is very minimal. We have far more work to do."

> *"Indeed, some scientists question the wisdom of advertising our presence. After all, maybe the aliens aren't exactly what you'd call warm and cuddly."*

Calling Out to Space Aliens Might Be Risky

Ilima Loomis

While there is some disagreement, most scientists think the odds are high that Earthlings are not the only intelligent beings in the universe. The real debate is how—or even whether—we should try to get in touch. In the following viewpoint, Ilima Loomis considers the potential risks of making ourselves known to beings we know nothing about. She also takes up the question of who should have the authority and responsibility for making decisions about how best to deal with this very delicate question. Loomis is a science journalist based in Hawaii.

"Should We Call Out to Space Aliens," Ilima Loomis, Science News for Students, March 21, 2017. Used with permission.

As you read, consider the following questions:

1. Invasions from hostile aliens are not the only risks Loomis mentions. What other potential hazards might be involved in making contact with alien civilizations?
2. How, according to this viewpoint, should the decision about whether or not to reach out to alien life be made?
3. Some experts quoted here think the question of whether or not to reach out to aliens is a moot point. Why do they say that?

Ever been to a party and wondered why no one was talking to you? That's kind of how SETI scientists feel—on a cosmic level.

For more than half a century, astronomers have been listening to space. They use powerful radio telescopes, hoping to pick up signals from civilizations in distant space. They call this project the Search for Extra-Terrestrial Intelligence, or SETI. The trouble is, they've never heard a single ping, beep or "howdy." The number of aliens who want to talk to us seems to be exactly zilch.

So how can we get the conversation started? Scientists disagree.

Some want to follow your mom's advice: Introduce yourself nicely. They think Earthlings should start beaming signals out into the universe. Maybe it would improve our chances of hearing back from aliens if we let them know we're friendly and want to chat.

This so-called "active SETI" would deliberately beam signals out in hopes of reaching space beings. Seth Shostak is an astronomer at the SETI Institute in Mountain View, Calif. He supports the idea. He also concedes that it is "extraordinarily controversial."

Indeed, some scientists question the wisdom of advertising our presence. After all, maybe the aliens aren't exactly what you'd call warm and cuddly. Do we really want to shout out to whomever will listen: "Here we are! Come invade our planet!"? At the very least, these scientists argue, people should discuss the idea and decide as a species whether we should try to actively put ourselves onto the radar screen of more technologically advanced beings.

"There are some people who think it's dangerous, because you don't know who's out there," Shostak says. "Maybe the aliens are just into yoga and poetry. But it could be that one percent of them are aggressive Klingons."

Shostak doesn't share these fears. But some people worry that if the aliens are not peaceable travelers, their response to even a friendly "hello" could be downright hostile. Some worry that instead of a friendly chat, those aliens might, as he puts it, "launch an attack and obliterate the Earth."

David Brin doesn't appreciate the Klingon jokes. He's a scientist and science fiction writer. He also is one of those people who argues that Earthlings should proceed with caution. It's not a matter of being afraid of some alien invasion, he says. "I know how unlikely those scenarios may be." Instead, he thinks of active SETI almost like a potential environmental hazard.

Broadcasting powerful signals would change the nature of our planet. It would make Earth more observable from space. Other projects must go through an environmental review, he says, and this should too. "What's so hard about that to understand?"

As an astrobiologist, David Grinspoon studies the possibilities of life throughout the universe. He works for the Planetary Science Institute in Washington, D.C. Whatever Earthlings do, Grinspoon thinks it's important for them to decide as a group.

"The more I think about it," he explains, "the more it seems almost anti-human to say, 'I'm just going to be the ambassador for the whole human race and start broadcasting to aliens on my own.'"

Alien Life Is Likely, Many Scientists Suspect

Inviting contact with space aliens might sound like the plot of one of Brin's sci-fi novels. Yet plenty of researchers are taking this idea quite seriously. Even though we haven't found extraterrestrials yet, many scientists believe that it's quite likely that life exists on other worlds.

For one thing, science recently has shown that planets are much more common than astronomers had once thought. There are probably billions of them in the universe.

Biology also has turned up plenty of life on Earth that can survive and thrive in extreme environments—conditions that once were thought uninhabitable. These include places that are very hot, very cold, very dry or even bathed in acid.

"Everything we've learned about other planets and the diversity of life on Earth points us in the direction of believing there is abundant life elsewhere in the universe," argues Grinspoon.

What's more, even if life truly needed many of the same conditions found on our world, planets have been turning up that may host Earth-like temperatures, atmospheres—and perhaps even water. Such worlds exist in what's known as "Goldilocks" zones. These are not too hot or too cold—but just right to sustain liquid water somewhere.

Whatever such alien life might be like—even if most of those organisms are just algae or worms—some would likely be intelligent, Grinspoon suspects. "It's not just a fantasy that someone might pick up a signal if we broadcast it," he says. "It's my belief that there probably are creatures out there. And some of them probably have much more advanced technology than we do."

Striking Up a Conversation

So how would people try to contact other worlds? Scientists have a few ideas. Like a message in a bottle, people could put something into a capsule and shoot it into space. Or scientists could flash lights at the aliens, training the beams of super-powerful lasers at nearby star systems. Think of it like Boy Scouts waving their flashlights at girls who might be camping on the other side of a lake. Researchers would send radio broadcasts out across the vast expanses of space.

Douglas Vakoch is president of METI International in San Francisco, Calif. (METI stands for Messaging Extraterrestrial Intelligence.) In addition to other ideas for sending out signals, he recommends beaming radio messages at other stars with huge radio telescopes, like the Arecibo (Air-eh-SEE-boh) observatory in Puerto Rico.

Right now, Arecibo uses radar to probe our solar system. The telescope sends out a pulse of radio waves. How long it takes those signals to bounce off things, such as asteroids, tells us how far away those things are. Under Vakoch's plan, the telescope would send out those same radar pulses. But he'd aim them at nearby star systems. If all went well, intelligent aliens would notice those radio tweets and answer our "beep" with a "boop."

"Maybe some civilizations out there are doing what we're doing," Vakoch says. "They're listening, but they're not transmitting." If they are, "we just wouldn't discover them," he notes. Active SETI, he explains, "is an attempt to let any civilization out there know not only that we're here, but also that we're interested in making contact."

So why do we even want to talk to aliens? The search for extraterrestrial intelligence—or ETI—is part of humanity's larger quest to explore the universe, and understand the nature of life, Vakoch says. "Perhaps more importantly, it holds a mirror up to ourselves."

Throughout human history, any time civilizations have met, they have exchanged ideas, knowledge and technology. Meeting a more advanced culture could give our species a new perspective about life on Earth, says Vakoch. It might also show us new tools to solve Earthly problems, he adds.

Brin sees it a bit differently: "It's worth bearing in mind that every time human civilizations that didn't know about each other came into contact, there was pain." Think about what happened to Native Americans or Africans when European explorers arrived on the scene, he says. Europeans coming to the "New World" brought along never-before-seen diseases. And their advanced technology, such as guns and metal, led to the destruction of the Native Americans' way of life.

That's one reason Brin thinks scientists and government leaders should not act too quickly. He advises that they think and talk it over before deciding what to do next. If we do contact aliens, studying our own history might give us ideas about ways to keep our interactions peaceful.

"Why did some contact situations [in history] go better than others?" Brin asks. "It turns out, there were some commonalities in the ones that were less painful. This should be something we study, not something we avoid."

E.T. May Already Know About Us

It's probably too late to hide from advanced space civilizations, many scientists observe. Supporters of active SETI point out that FM radio and television signals both emit a high enough frequency that they could be picked up in space. Then there are all of those signals flying around between satellites, and those powerful radar pings from telescopes like Arecibo.

While people debate the issue, maybe the aliens are already watching our TV shows and listening to our music, says Philip Lubin. He's a physicist at the University of California, Santa Barbara. "When someone says we shouldn't transmit," he notes, "you kind of have to say, 'Okay, what planet do you live on?' Because we've been transmitting for 100 years."

Active SETI would take those transmissions to the next level. It would beam out more powerful signals, focusing them on the closest star systems. "The real question," Lubin asks, "is should we transmit with the intention of being understood?"

Any civilization so advanced that it could visit Earth would already have the technology to pick up our signals, Vakoch agrees. So it would likely already know we're here. In that case, he cautions: Maybe it's in the best interest of the people of Earth to offer a peaceable greeting before those aliens pay us a visit. "There's the idea that doing something is more dangerous than doing nothing," Vakoch says. "But maybe it's more dangerous not to say anything."

He doesn't want to wait to start active SETI. He does, however, agree that society should talk openly about the search for extraterrestrial life—and decide what to do if aliens respond. Most scientists have agreed to the "Protocols for an ETI Signal Detection." This is a plan for what to do if aliens make contact with us. (Step one: Tell other scientists so they can confirm the discovery.) But Vakoch would like to see those policies debated and agreed to by the United Nations.

He concedes, though, "So far, we haven't convinced [U.N. officials] that this should be at the top of their list."

Grinspoon does think we should debate the issue before we broadcast messages into space. But it's not because he's afraid of ET. Discussing the welfare and future of our planet "is the kind of thing we humans need to get better at," he says. In fact, the biggest threat to human civilization isn't alien invasion, he argues. It's things like climate change, war and pollution.

The only solution to those problems is to learn how to think and act not as different races and countries, but as one species, he says. "It's actually more important to try to have a conversation with our fellow human beings than it is to have a conversation with aliens," he says. "That is our survival challenge."

| *"If anything, intelligent life is a fluke in our universe, the exception and not the rule."*

There's Probably Not Much Out There

Marcelo Gleiser

In the following viewpoint Marcelo Gleiser takes a different view from the scientists quoted in the previous viewpoint. Reacting to a claim made by Stephen Hawking regarding life and creation, the author argues that life in the universe is rare. However, it is important to note that Gleiser is talking about complex, multicellular life. Intelligent life, he says, is a fluke. He makes a detailed explanation for why he thinks so. Gleiser is professor of physics and astronomy at Dartmouth University.

As you read, consider the following questions:

1. How did oxygen-breathing life forms come to dominate life on Earth?
2. What is one theory mentioned here about the development of multicellular life forms?
3. How does Gleiser say that his discussion of this issue illustrates the way science works?

"How Rare Is Life?" by Marcelo Gleiser, National Public Radio Inc., September 15, 2010. Reprinted by permission.

I n my post last week on Hawking's claim that science has shown that God is unnecessary to explain Creation, I made a comment about life:

> Furthermore, Hawking also claims that the universe is "just right" for generating living beings like us. Instead, I argue that life is rare (take a look around our solar system neighbors for starters and then look at the history of life on Earth, and all that had to happen for multicellular organisms to thrive) and that complex, intelligent life much rarer still. If anything, intelligent life is a fluke in our universe, the exception and not the rule.

A large number of readers reacted to this, essentially claiming that I had no observational grounds to make this sort of claim. Today, I'd like to revisit the issue, which is not only of great importance—Are we alone?—but also reveals how science works, by careful analysis of available data and the testing of hypotheses.

First, note that my comment was not about life but about complex, intelligent life. There is a huge difference! Simple life may be abundant. Indeed, what we know of the only sample of life— planet Earth—indicates that given the right conditions, life finds its way to emerge. Earth formed some 4.5 billion years ago from the same nebula that gave rise to the sun and all other planets of the solar system. During the first 600 or 700 million years, Earth was a veritable hell, constantly bombarded by the debris left over from the formation of the planets and their moons. Under these conditions, life was impossible. Earth didn't have a solid crust and its surface would constantly melt due to the energy of the violent impacts.

At around 3.9 billion years ago, things got relatively quiet. Simple chemicals reacted and by 3.5 billion years ago, the first simple life forms were swimming in Earth's shallow ancient oceans. Some scientists would claim that even by 3.8 billion years ago there were signs of life, but these findings remain controversial. Even if we take the 3.5 billion years ago as a starting point, we can state that life on Earth formed within a few hundred million

We Now Have the Tools to Talk to, Not Just Listen for, Alien Life

Is it time to take the search for intelligent aliens to the next level?

For more than half a century, scientists have been scanning the heavens for signals generated by intelligent alien life. They haven't found anything conclusive yet, so some researchers are advocating adding an element called "active SETI" (search for extraterrestrial intelligence) — not just listening, but also beaming out transmissions of our own designed to catch aliens' eyes.

Active SETI "may just be the approach that lets us make contact with life beyond Earth," Douglas Vakoch, director of interstellar message composition at the SETI Institute in Mountain View, California, said earlier this month during a panel discussion at the annual meeting of the American Association for the Advancement of Science (AAAS) in San Jose.

"Should Humanity Try to Contact Alien Civilizations?" by Mike Wall, Space. com, February 24, 2015.

years, which is quite fast in planetary scales. So simple life may be fairly easy to assemble. What about complex life?

These were prokaryotes, primitive cells with exposed genetic material. More modern cells, like the eukaryotes we are made of, have the genetic material protected in sacs (the DNA is in a nucleus). The prokaryotes reigned supreme for about two billion years. Only then (numbers are rounded up here) eukaryotic cells appeared. As I discussed in another blog on sponges and creationism, sponge-like multicellular creatures only appeared some 500 to 700 million years ago, give or take a couple of hundred million years.

That is, for about three billion years, life on Earth was only in the form of single-celled organisms.

The transition from unicellular to multicellular life forms remains unclear. Given what we know from natural selection, quite possibly cell colonies found it advantageous to gather together—united we win!—and function as a whole being. Or some ate the other and formed a joint being. However, it's clear that when we study the history of life on Earth we can't separate it from the history of Earth itself. As a planet, Earth co-evolved with life. For example, the single-celled blue-green algae that populated Earth's primitive oceans discovered photosynthesis (accidentally of course), the ability to use the sun's light to create the energy they needed to survive. With this, they emitted oxygen, a gas that didn't exist in Earth's primitive atmosphere for about 2 billion years. It was this surplus of oxygen that allowed for more efficient metabolic pathways which, eventually, led to more complex life forms.

In a very real sense, we are here because our distant unicellular ancestors learned to exhale oxygen.

So, when we ponder on the existence of complex multicellular life in the cosmos we must take into account the conditions that are favorable for complex life to not only form but to survive for long times. It's not just a question of having liquid water and the right chemicals. (These, of course, are a must.) The planet must have a stable orbit and relatively stable temperatures. In the case of the Earth, the reason why we have four seasons and temperatures that don't vary like crazy is that we have a large moon. The moon stabilizes the tilt of the Earth (the Earth is like an inclined spinning top with a tilt of 23.5 degrees from the vertical), allowing for stable seasons and liquid water for billions of years. Had the moon been lighter, the Earth's axis would wobble randomly, oceans could freeze for long periods of time, and complex life would be very hard-pressed to survive.

Earth also has two very important "blankets" that protect life from the nasty and lethal radiation that constantly rains from the skies. Earth's magnetic field funnels electrically-charged particles coming from the sun into the poles. Sometimes, we see them as auroras at high latitudes. Also, the ozone layer protects us from nasty UV radiation from the sun. Living near a star is no picnic.

Some of these arguments were masterfully developed in the book *Rare Earth* by Peter Ward and Donald Brownlee published in 2000. There are other arguments that we don't have the space to address. In my last book, *A Tear at the Edge of Creation*, I updated their arguments, placing them in the context of what we know now.

Finally, the jump from multicellular to complex multicellular and intelligent life is also a fluke. Just think that intelligence emerged only very recently, some 3.5 billion years after life emerged. It's common to think that intelligence and even complexity is a natural consequence of evolution, that is, if there is life give it enough time and it will turn smart.

That's not what natural selection tells us. All life cares about is being well-adapted to the changing planetary environment. (And by the way, that's only possible because genetic reproduction allows for mutations to occur. Had it been perfect, life would fail.) Think of the dumb and fearsome dinosaurs that were here happy for 150 million years. No intelligence there, just good adaptation.

Surely, given the enormous number of other planets and moons out there in the galaxy (and in the hundreds of billions of other galaxies!) and the fact that the laws of chemistry and physics apply throughout the cosmos, life should not be an Earthly phenomenon. But whatever life forms exist out there, given what we know of how life evolved here on Earth and the many conditions that come into play in order to sustain complex life, it's a huge jump to assume that complex life is equally widespread. Intelligent life even more so. I could also use the fact that we haven't been visited by aliens and explore Fermi's paradox, but I'll leave that for another day. But even if there are other intelligent life forms in the galaxy, and we can't either prove or rule that out with the evidence at hand, the reality is that for practical purposes we are alone and will probably be for the foreseeable future.

> *"One of the smartest men on the planet, Stephen Hawking…believes that our messages might attract unwanted attention from unsavory creatures looking to blast us back into the stone age."*

They Probably Already Know We're Here

Andrew Fain

In the previous viewpoint Marcelo Gleiser made the case for why he thinks intelligent life is rare in the universe. In the following viewpoint Andrew Fain argues just the opposite. Using colorful, easy to understand examples, Fain explains several reasons we might not have made contact yet, even if there are plenty of others out there. In the end, however, he says that we need not bother with the debate about whether or not to reach out to aliens. They will get in touch with us soon enough. NOTE: Physicist and cosmologist Stephen Hawking, to whom Fain refers in this viewpoint, died in 2018. Fain is a science writer who specializes in the search for extraterrestrial intelligence.

"Why Haven't We Found Any Aliens Yet?" by Andrew Fain, Phys.org, August 11, 2016.

As you read, consider the following questions:

1. The author makes several arguments for why we haven't made contact with alien intelligence even if there's plenty of it out there. Do you find these arguments convincing? Do they successfully refute Gleiser's arguments in the previous viewpoint?
2. What logical flaw does Fain find in the Fermi paradox?
3. If Fain is correct, do you think humans should continue the search for extraterrestrial intelligence? Why or why not?

M any years ago, Carl Sagan predicted there could be as many as 10,000 advanced extraterrestrial civilizations in our galaxy.

After nearly 60 years of searching without success, a growing list of scientists believe life on Earth only came about because of a lucky series of evolutionary accidents, a long list of improbable events that just happened to come together at the right time and will never be repeated. Is it possible they are right and we are all there is? Highly unlikely.

Earth is a typical rocky planet, in an average solar system, nestled in the spiral arm of an ordinary galaxy. All the events and elements that came together to build our world could happen almost everywhere throughout the galaxy and there should be nothing unusual about the evolution of life on this planet or any others.

In a galaxy of hundreds of billions of stars, the law of averages dictates that intelligent life must exist somewhere. So, why haven't we found it yet? There could be many reasons.

Looking for a radio signal in a galaxy of over 400 billion worlds across 100,000 light years and billions of radio frequencies makes the proverbial needle in a haystack sound easy. Imagine you are driving home, your spouse in one car and you in the other. There's a thick fog making visual confirmation impossible and no cell phone reception. Luckily, a week ago you had a 250 channel CB installed in both cars. Unfortunately, you forgot to agree on a broadcast channel. To chat, the two CBs would have to be on at the same time and you'd need to independently search every channel, listen, broadcast, then move to the next, hoping to get lucky enough to land on the same channel.

What are the odds that would happen? Not very good. Multiply this scenario one hundred billion times and you have some idea of the challenges facing SETI. To add to that, advanced civilizations probably only stay radio active for a relatively short time in their development as they develop more sophisticated technology. Searching the radio spectrum would require looking at one frequency 24/7 for years to be sure you weren't missing something and telescope time is far too expensive for that. While you were sitting on that single frequency, 20 extraterrestrial signals could have come in on other channels and you'd never know it.

The Fermi paradox is used by many skeptics as the holy grail when trying to prove there is nobody out there. Fermi theorized that a galaxy with so much potential for life must be full of extraterrestrials. He noted that since the majority of stars are considerably older than our sun, extraterrestrials could be millions of years more advanced than us. Fermi calculated that even at sub light speed one of those civilizations should have colonized the galaxy by now and we would have seen evidence of it.

There is, however, a problem with that logic.

In 50,000 years, humans will probably look a little different than people do now. In 10 million years, considerably different. Imagine a civilization completely different from us from the start and 10 million years more advanced. We might not even be able to recognize them as life forms, let alone see any evidence of their existence.

Arthur C. Clarke once said advanced extraterrestrials would probably be indistinguishable to us from magic. Their communications would be like listening for an answer to drumbeats and getting only silence while the ether around you is filled with more information in a second than one could utter in a lifetime.

There could be the alien equivalent of the super bowl going on a few light years away and we would probably not even have a clue.

The distances in our galaxy are incredibly vast. Current spacecraft travel about 20 times faster than the speed of a bullet. While that sounds fast, at that speed it would take a spacecraft 75,000 years to travel to our nearest star only 4 light years away. Light years are a measure of distance so if we could speed that ship up to 186,000 miles per second it would take 4 years to reach that same star.

Looking at a star 1,000 light years away is like being in a time machine. You are not seeing it as it is now, but one thousand years ago. Our galaxy is about 100,000 light years across with over 200 billion stars. Current theory suggests there may be as many as one billion earth-like planets in our galaxy. If just one tenth of those had some kind of life, that would leave us with about 100 million worlds harboring one-celled creatures or better.

If just the tiniest fraction of them, (one one hundred thousandth) managed to spawn an advanced race of beings, there could be as many as 1,000 extraterrestrial civilizations in our galaxy. Regardless of whether you consider that a lot or a little, that would mean one technically advanced alien society exists for every hundred million stars. Our nearest extraterrestrial neighbor might be very, very far away. In the movies, the speculative fiction of warp speed, hyper drive and worm holes enable spaceships to travel faster than the speed of light and breach those distances fairly easily. But if the physics of this turns out to be impossible, then even the nearest alien civilizations may find interstellar travel very difficult and quite undesirable.

Another reason extraterrestrials may have made themselves scarce could be that the galaxy is jam packed with all sorts of weird beings and wondrous destinations. In this scenario why would advanced forms of life want to come here? There are probably so many more interesting places to visit. It would be like hunting for an exotic bird and not even giving the ant hill below your feet a second look.

Stephen Hawking has said, "I believe extraterrestrial life is quite common in the universe, although intelligent life less so. Some say it has yet to appear on Earth."

Many think once a civilization achieves radio, it has a short window of but a few hundred years before it starts to integrate artificial intelligence into its own biology. Machines do everything so much easier, with far less risk and are immortal. It is entirely possible any aliens we hear from will have morphed into something more machine like than biological.

There has been a push lately for SETI to expand its operations from just passively listening, to actively broadcasting messages into the cosmos. One of the smartest men on the planet, Stephen Hawking, doesn't think that's a good idea. He believes that our messages might attract unwanted attention from unsavory creatures looking to blast us back into the stone age. He uses what happened to the Native Americans when they first encountered Columbus as an example. Alien races may have had to endure the same aggressive survival of the fittest culture. If they are at least as smart as Stephen Hawking, than everyone out there could be listening and nobody is broadcasting for fear of attracting the equivalent of Darth Vader and the Evil Empire to their shores.

Or, maybe there is a signal on its way right now, having traveled thousand of years, arriving next week, month or year.

Many scientists like Paul Davies, think SETI needs to start thinking more out of the box in its search methods. He advocates analyzing places in our own solar system like the moon, planets, asteroids and the Earth for evidence that aliens have passed this way. We should also be open to the possibility that we have already received a message from the stars and don't recognize it because it arrived by something other than radio. Physist Vladimir Charbak thinks that life may have been spread throughout the galaxy by intelligent design and there may actually be evidence of this within our own DNA just waiting to be discovered.

Another reason we have yet to detect alien life could be there is nothing out there to find. Or to put it another way, we are the only game in town. To best answer that question, ask yourself, does this seem logical? There is a very good chance that one or more worlds just in our own solar system harbor some form of life. In a galaxy with as many as one billion or more potentially habitable planets, one could almost guarantee many of them will host life. There may potentially be hundreds of millions of worlds with living things on them. Does it make sense that in all that habitable real estate we are the only race to evolve into an intelligent species?

We humans tend to think of things with a distinctly anthropomorphic spin. Notions like, life needs water, oxygen and is based on carbon. Or, an advanced alien race would use radio and their signals should repeat. In popular culture, extraterrestrials portrayed in movies look remotely like us. This is done so we can recognize emotions and that fills movie theaters. I can remember aliens portrayed in the classic science fiction television show, "The Outer Limits" as energy balls, dust motes and tumbleweeds. They weren't the most popular episodes, but the reality is that those portrayals are probably closer to the truth than ET and his heart lamp. Extraterrestrials will probably be as different from us as we are from a blade of grass and their motivations a complete mystery. It is very possible that the reason we haven't found them yet is one that completely eludes our understanding at this point.

So where does that leave us?

Time and patience.

If you compare the 4.5 billion year old earth to a 24 hour clock, mankind doesn't appear until a little over a minute before midnight. Take the almost sixty years we have been looking for extraterrestrials and project that on the same clock, it probably represents only about 20 or 30 seconds worth of searching for intelligent beings who may have been around millions and perhaps billions of years longer than we have. Our passage through time is just a tiny almost imperceptible blip when compared to the evolution of our galaxy.

New, very powerful listening devices will be coming into operation soon as well as sophisticated instruments that will be able to analyze exoplanets atmospheres to look for hints of life. SETI will expand into new areas and scientists will be able to devote a lot more telescope time to the search as the newly funded (100MM) Project Breakthough Listen kicks into high gear. It will cover 10 times more of the sky and the entire 1-10GHz radio spectrum. There will be more powerful optical and infrared searches and it is estimated the project will generate in a day as much data as SETI produced in an entire year. Recently, Project Breakthrough Starshot was announced as well. Seeded by another 100MM by Russian Billionaire, Yuri Milner, this ambitious project seeks to send a tiny light propelled robotic spacecraft to our nearest star system, Alpha Centauri. Stephen Hawking thinks this can be accomplished within the next generation and that new technology would allow a journey of only 20 years.

SETI scientist Nathalie Cabrol thinks its also time for a new approach to SETI's search, a reboot if you will. She feels that "SETI's vision has been constrained by whether ET has technology that resembles or thinks like us. She feels that the search, so far, has in essence been a search for ourselves. Electromagnetic fingerprints of radio transmitions carry a strong like us assumption." She proposes involving a lot more disciplines in a redesign of the search. Astrobiology, life sciences, geoscience, cognitive science and mathematics among others. Her plan is to invite the research community to help craft a new scientific roadmap for SETI that very well may redefine the meaning of life and the cosmic search for new forms of it.

Some experts say we won't see evidence of extraterrestrials for another 1500 years. That's the time it will take for our TV and radio signals to have reached enough stars and have the best chance to be discovered.

In my opinion, I think highly advanced extraterrestrial societies already know we're here and in about 10-15 years we'll start getting some of the answers we've been looking for.

> *"One possible answer to Fermi's Paradox is that civilizations don't last very long. But some techno-signatures might remain even after a civilization ends."*

They Might Already Be Dead

Adam Frank

Where previous viewpoint arguments have been based mostly on logic and not a small amount of speculation, in the following viewpoint Adam Frank argues that we now have data and evidence to search for technological civilizations—not just biomarkers that indicate some form of life. If the author is right, whether or not to make contact might again be a moot point, since the civilizations we find using these methods might very likely be already extinct. Frank is a physicist and astronomer who is active in the relatively new field of astrobiology, the study of life in the universe.

"Is Humanity Unusual in The Cosmos?" by Adam Frank, National Public Radio Inc., April 2, 2018. Reprinted by permission.

As you read, consider the following questions:

1. What new scientific methods does Frank discuss that could make the search for extraterrestrial life easier?
2. What is an example of a "techno-signature" mentioned in this viewpoint?
3. In this viewpoint the author says that one possible answer to Fermi's paradox is that advanced civilizations don't last very long. If that is the case, can you think of a reason it might be beneficial to locate these "dead" civilizations?

W e're entering uncharted territory.
For more than 2,000 years, we humans have been arguing about life and, in particular, intelligent life in the universe. But arguing was pretty much where it always ended.

For all that time, we never had any evidence or any data that could raise the discussion above two people with different opinions yelling at each other.

But this era may well be nearing its end.

The "exoplanet" revolution of the last 20 years has shown us that the universe is awash in alien worlds. More exciting, we now have methods where the atmospheres of those worlds may provide indirect evidence—called "bio-signatures"—for the existence of life.

Over the next few decades we may finally have data relevant to the question of other life in the universe.

But what if we want to ask about intelligence? What about alien civilizations—or, as I like to call them, "exo-civilizations"? This is something I have been thinking about a lot over the last few years (it's the subject of my new book). In carrying out my own studies, I have often been drawn to the work of Harvard astrophysicist Avi Loeb.

Loeb works on a variety of subjects, including black holes and early cosmic history. But together with collaborator Manasvi Lingam, Loeb has carried out work that is simultaneously deep and expansive on the topic of astrobiology and exo-civilizations.

When we think of aliens and science, we usual usually think of the Search of Extraterrestrial Intelligence (SETI). This has often meant radio telescopes being used to search for messages purposely beamed at us from an exo-civilization. But unlike these kinds of purposeful signals, a "techno-signature" is an unintentional marker of the civilization's existence. With the discovery of so many exo-planets, astronomers will now be spending a lot time staring at these other worlds in many different wavelengths of light (not just radio). This is how they hope to find bio-signatures.

But what about techno-signatures?

Loeb and Lingam have explored a number of different ways we might find markers of another civilization. What, for example, would be the consequences of a civilization covering large portions of its planet in solar cells to generate power? Lingam and Loeb have shown that light reflected from such a planet would carry a "signal" of all that silicon on the planet's surface, making it an intriguing example of a techno-signature.

Over the past couple weeks, I had a chance to ask Loeb some questions about what we should be thinking about when we consider exo-civilizations. With regard to techno-signatures, Loeb was quick to point out that a civilization need not be alive now for us to find its techno-signatures.

"There is, of course, Fermi's paradox, which asks where is everybody," Loeb said. One possible answer to Fermi's paradox is that civilizations don't last very long. But some techno-signatures might remain even after a civilization ends. "It's possible that when we survey planets we may find artifacts of dead civilizations that aren't around anymore," Loeb added.

Planet-spanning solar panels offer one example of such possible artifacts, since they could still exist on planet's surface long after the civilization that built them collapsed.

One of the most intriguing ideas Loeb raised was that the most common kinds of techno-signatures might not be things we have the sensitivity to find yet. Pointing to what's happening with Elon

Musk and Jeff Bezos and their space efforts, Loeb said, "Eventually we may have the ability to launch a lot of things into space."

Once a civilization becomes truly interplanetary, there will be many artifacts existing in space rather than on planets. Loeb calls these physical objects "messages in a bottle" because if we had enough sensitivity, we might be able to see them. "These things would be very difficult to detect because they would be putting out very low power," Loeb said.

Loeb pointed to the recent discovery of 'Oumuamua, an asteroid from another star system that was caught wandering through our own. Our ability to find 'Oumuamua depended on advances in telescope technology. When it comes to techno-signatures, Loeb wonders if, perhaps, there might be spacecraft from other civilizations out there, too.

"The interstellar medium might be full of these things but how would we find them?" Loeb asked.

In his comments to me, Loeb pointed to the detection of gravitational waves, the ripples in space and time predicted by Einstein's theory of relativity. It took many decades for scientists to develop instruments sensitive enough to detect these signals that come from things like colliding black holes. The gravitational-wave example shows how detection of anything depends technological advances. So when it comes to techno-signatures, as our technologies gets better we might suddenly find lots of signals from the activity of technological civilizations.

Loeb is essentially optimistic about the search.

"We humans are probably not special," he said, explaining that with so many planets in the universe, the rise of civilizations may not be so usual.

But Loeb's belief that we are "not special" takes a back seat to his scientific dedication to data.

"I give the final say to the facts," he said. So, for Loeb, the effort now should be developing search technologies and strategies so we can just go out and look.

And that's what makes our moment in history so unique. We are poised to start staring at exo-planets and their environments in all kinds of new ways.

What do you think we're going to find?

> *"I don't think you can put human views on to [aliens]; that's a dangerous way of thinking. Aliens are alien. If they exist at all, we cannot assume they're like us."*

It's Too Late to Hide

Alok Jha

Previous authors have mentioned scientist Stephen Hawking's warning that trying to contact alien civilizations would be foolhardy. In the following viewpoint Alok Jha takes a close look at Hawking's claim to find a counterargument. The author talks with other scientists, who think the risk is minimal because we are unlikely to have any resources of interest to a civilization advanced enough to be capable of interstellar travel. Also, the author points out, our radio broadcast signals have probably already given us away. Jha has been a science correspondent for the Guardian *and the* BBC, *and now for the* Economist.

"Is Stephen Hawking Right About Aliens?" by Alok Jha, Guardian News and Media Limited, April 30, 2010. Reprinted by permission.

As you read, consider the following questions:

1. What, according to this author, is the first thing we need to do if we wish to hide from aliens?
2. Why is it so difficult for humans to imagine what alien life might be like? How do our prejudices limit our thinking about possibilities for alien life?
3. This viewpoint ends on an amusing, but oddly reassuring note. What do you make of that last point? Do you find it hopeful or troubling that if aliens have discovered us, it is primarily our popular culture that they've encountered?

In February 2008, NASA sent the Beatles song, "Across the Universe," across the universe. Pointing the telescopes in its Deep Space Network towards the north star, Polaris, astronomers played out their short cosmic DJ set, hoping that it might be heard by intelligent aliens during its 430-year journey to the star.

The hunt for intelligent species outside Earth may be a staple of literature and film—but it is happening in real life, too. NASA probes are on the lookout for planets outside our solar system, and astronomers are carefully listening for any messages being beamed through space. How awe-inspiring it would be to get confirmation that we are not alone in the universe, to finally speak to an alien race. Wouldn't it?

Well no, according to the eminent physicist Stephen Hawking. "If aliens visit us, the outcome would be much as when Columbus landed in America, which didn't turn out well for the Native Americans," Hawking has said in a forthcoming documentary made for the Discovery Channel. He argues that, instead of trying to find and communicate with life in the cosmos, humans would be better off doing everything they can to avoid contact.

Hawking believes that, based on the sheer number of planets that scientists know must exist, we are not the only life-form in the universe. There are, after all, billions and billions of stars in our galaxy alone, with, it is reasonable to expect, an even greater number of planets orbiting them. And it is not unreasonable to expect some of that alien life to be intelligent, and capable of interstellar communication. So, when someone with Hawking's knowledge of the universe advises against contact, it's worth listening, isn't it?

Seth Shostak, a senior astronomer at the Seti Institute in California, the world's leading organisation searching for telltale alien signals, is not so sure. "This is an unwarranted fear," Shostak says. "If their interest in our planet is for something valuable that our planet has to offer, there's no particular reason to worry about them now. If they're interested in resources, they have ways of finding rocky planets that don't depend on whether we broadcast or not. They could have found us a billion years ago."

If we were really worried about shouting in the stellar jungle, Shostak says, the first thing to do would be to shut down the BBC, NBC, CBS and the radars at all airports. Those broadcasts have been streaming into space for years—the oldest is already more than 80 light years from Earth—so it is already too late to stop passing aliens watching every episode of *Big Brother* or *What Katie and Peter Did Next*.

The biggest and most active hunt for life outside Earth started in 1960, when Frank Drake pointed the Green Bank radio telescope in West Virginia towards the star Tau Ceti. He was looking for anomalous radio signals that could have been sent by intelligent life. Eventually, his idea turned into SETI (standing for Search for Extra Terrestrial Intelligence), which used the downtime on radar telescopes around the world to scour the sky for any signals. For 50 years, however, the sky has been silent.

There are lots of practical problems involved in hunting for aliens, of course, chief among them being distance. If our nearest neighbours were life-forms on the (fictional) forest moon of Endor, 1,000 light years away, it would take a millennium for us to receive any message they might send. If the Endorians were watching us, the light reaching them from Earth at this very moment would show them our planet as it was 1,000 years ago; in Europe that means lots of fighting between knights around castles and, in north America, small bands of natives living on the great plains. It is not a timescale that allows for quick banter—and, anyway, they might not be communicating in our direction.

The lack of a signal from ET has not, however, prevented astronomers and biologists (not to mention film-makers) coming up with a whole range of ideas about what aliens might be like. In the early days of SETI, astronomers focused on the search for planets like ours—the idea being that, since the only biology we know about is our own, we might as well assume aliens are going to be something like us. But there's no reason why that should be true. You don't even need to step off the Earth to find life that is radically different from our common experience of it.

"Extremophiles" are species that can survive in places that would quickly kill humans and other "normal" life-forms. These single-celled creatures have been found in boiling hot vents of water thrusting through the ocean floor, or at temperatures well below the freezing point of water. The front ends of some creatures that live near deep-sea vents are 200C warmer than their back ends.

"In our naive and parochial way, we have named these things extremophiles, which shows prejudice—we're normal, everything else is extreme," says Ian Stewart, a mathematician at Warwick University and author of *What Does A Martian Look Like?* "From the point of view of a creature that lives in boiling water, we're extreme because we live in much milder temperatures. We're at least as extreme compared to them as they are compared to us."

On Earth, life exists in water and on land but, on a giant gas planet, for example, it might exist high in the atmosphere, trapping nutrients from the air swirling around it. And given that aliens may be so out of our experience, guessing motives and intentions if they ever got in touch seems beyond the realms even of Hawking's mind.

Paul Davies, an astrophysicist at Arizona State University and chair of SETI's post-detection taskforce, argues that alien brains, with their different architecture, would interpret information very differently from ours. What we think of as beautiful or friendly might come across as violent to them, or vice versa. "Lots of people think that because they would be so wise and knowledgeable, they would be peaceful," adds Stewart. "I don't think you can assume that. I don't think you can put human views on to them; that's a dangerous way of thinking. Aliens are alien. If they exist at all, we cannot assume they're like us."

Answers to some of these conundrums will begin to emerge in the next few decades. The researchers at the forefront of the work are astrobiologists, working in an area that has steadily marched in from the fringes of science thanks to the improvements in technology available to explore space.

Scientists discovered the first few extrasolar planets in the early 1990s and, ever since, the numbers have shot up. Today, scientists know of 443 planets orbiting around more than 350 stars. Most are gas giants in the mould of Jupiter, the smallest being Gliese 581, which has a mass of 1.9 Earths. In 2009, NASA launched the Kepler satellite, a probe specifically designed to look for Earth-like planets.

Future generations of ground-based telescopes, such as the proposed European Extremely Large Telescope (with a 30m main mirror), could be operational by 2030, and would be powerful enough to image the atmospheres of faraway planets, looking for chemical signatures that could indicate life. The SETI Institute also, finally, has a serious piece of kit under construction: the Allen Array (funded by a $11.5m/£7.5m donation from Microsoft co-founder Paul Allen) has, at present, 42 radio antennae, each six metres in diameter, but there are plans, if the SETI Institute can raise another $35m, to have up to 300 radio dishes.

In all the years that SETI has been running, it has managed to look carefully at less than 1,000 star systems. With the full Allen Array, they could look at 1,000 star systems in a couple of years.

Shostak is confident that, as telescope technology keeps improving, SETI will find an ET signal within the next two decades. "We will have looked at another million star systems in two dozen years. If this is going to work, it will work soon."

And what happens if and when we detect a signal? "My strenuous advice will be that the coordinates of the transmitting entity should be kept confidential, until the world community has had a chance to evaluate what it's dealing with," Davies told the *Guardian* recently. "We don't want anybody just turning a radio telescope on the sky and sending their own messages to the source."

But his colleague, Shostak, says we should have no such concerns. "You'll have told the astronomical community—that's thousands of people. Are you going to ask them all not to tell anybody where you're pointing your antenna? There's no way you could do that.

"And anyway, why wouldn't you tell them where [the alien lifeform] is? Are you afraid people will broadcast their own message? They might do that but, remember, *The Gong Show* has already been broadcast for years." And, for that matter, the Beatles.

Periodical and Internet Sources Bibliography

The following articles have been selected to supplement the diverse views presented in this chapter.

David P. Barash, "Anthropic Arrogance: Claims that the Universe is Designed for Humans Raise Far More Troubling Questions than They Can Possibly Answer," Aeon, 18 September 2018. https://aeon.co/essays/why-a-human-centred-universe-is-not-a-humane-one.

Nadia Drake, "How Would We React to Finding Aliens? Perhaps Not the Way You'd Expect," *National Geographic*, February 16, 2018. https://news.nationalgeographic.com/2018/02/how-would-people-react-alien-life-discovery-aaas-space-science.

Adam Frank, "How Do Aliens Solve Climate Change?" *The Atlantic*, May 30, 2018. https://www.theatlantic.com/science/archive/2018/05/how-do-aliens-solve-climate-change/561479.

———. "Was There a Civilization on Earth Before Humans?" *The Atlantic*, April 13, 2018.

Robert H. Gray, "The Fermi Paradox Is Not Fermi's, and It Is Not a Paradox," *Scientific American* (guest blog), January 29, 2016.

Michael Greshko, "How Would Aliens Detect Life on Earth?" *National Geographic*, March 26, 2018. https://news.nationalgeographic.com/2018/03/how-aliens-could-discover-life-on-earth-one-strange-rock-science.

Lisa Grossman, "We Probably Won't Hear from Aliens. But by the Time We Do, They'll Be Dead," *Science News*, March 12, 2018. https://www.sciencenews.org/article/drake-equation-alien-extraterrestrial-civilizations.

William Herkewitz, "If Aliens Contact Us, We Won't Understand," Astronomy, May 1, 2017. http://astronomy.com/bonus/alien-contact.

Elizabeth Howell, "How Would Humanity React If We Really Found Aliens?" April 30, 2018, Space.com. https://www.space.com/40435-finding-aliens-humanity-reaction.html.

Samuel Levin, "Proof of Life: How Would We Recognise an Alien if We Saw One?" *Aeon*, 10 October 2018. https://aeon.co/ideas /proof-of-life-how-would-we-recognise-an-alien-if-we-saw-one.

Steve Mirsky, "Intelligent Aliens May Know About Us Well Before We Find Out About Them," *Scientific American,* January 1, 2018. https://www.scientificamerican.com/article/intelligent-aliens -may-know-about-us-well-before-we-find-out-about-them.

Matt Reynolds, "The Almighty Tussle over Whether We Should Talk to Aliens or Not," *Wired*, 26 September 2018. https://www.wired .co.uk/article/messaging-aliens-seti-meti.

Molly Roberts, "The Aliens Are Coming, and No One Cares," *Washington Post*, December 19, 2017. https://www .washingtonpost.com/blogs/post-partisan/wp/2017/12/19/the -aliens-are-coming-and-no-one-cares/?utm _term=.475e711fa05e.

Seth Shostak, "We Just Beamed a Signal at Space Aliens. Was That a Bad Idea?" NBC News MACH, November 20, 2017. https://www. nbcnews.com/mach/science/we-just-beamed-signal-space -aliens-was-bad-idea-ncna822446.

OPPOSING
VIEWPOINTS®
SERIES

CHAPTER 3

Is Space Exploration a Public Good?

Chapter Preface

While we dither about the potential consequences of making first contact, space exploration is continuing. It would be more accurate, and perhaps more apt, to say that it is rebooting. Modern space exploration is very different from the Cold War space race, and as such, it presents very different demands and difficulties. The process raises many questions beyond what will happen when and if we meet ET. Of course there are plenty of other potential issues, such as those discussed in Chapter One. But fundamentally, today's space race is a function of our times, its economic arrangements and political alignments.

One of the primary differences between the space race of the 1960s and 70s (space race 1.0) and the modern version (space race 2.0) is that the race is no longer between two superpower nations competing to create the most enviable technology and the most formidable military. It is, as are most things in the modern age, very often about making the most money, whether that be for a private company or a nation. That is not to say that national interest no longer plays a role. It most certainly does. As one of this chapter's viewpoints stresses, many nations are jumping into the space race with the aim of improving their own economies as well as getting a leg up on the potential military uses of space, whether those be for defense or aggression.

Another difference between space exploration then and now is that the unexpected benefits, such as major innovations in computer technology, materials science, and even medicine, are no longer unexpected. Anyone who has been paying attention to the history of space exploration knows that the extreme innovation and experimentation required for a successful space program will provide unimagined side benefits. The economics are not necessarily simpler, but that they are a prime consideration is beyond debate.

The authors of the viewpoints in the following chapter explore various economic and political considerations of the future of space exploration. First up is a viewpoint that argues that government investment in innovative technologies, such as those required for space exploration, is crucial.

> *"If any and all human life is valuable for its own sake, then we have a duty to generate more of it ... Under such a moral imperative, humanity has no choice but to forge new frontiers for expansion. Space, with its nearly infinite possibilities for new places for human life to flourish, is the only real frontier left."*

Space Exploration Is a Moral Imperative

E. R. Klein

In the following viewpoint E. R. Klein argues that a commitment to humanity requires the exploration and development of new frontiers that would allow the growth and furthering of the human population. The author uses the philosophies of such figures as Roy Weatherford and Aldo Leopold to make the case that Earth is a crowded place with finite and depleted resources. To continue evolving and expanding we must colonize space. Klein is careful, however, to note that this view should not obscure the fact that we should continue to make efforts to improve life on Earth. Klein's article on the moral obligation for space exploration was originally published in 2003, and the position was subsequently advocated by the late Dr. Stephen Hawking, who held the Lucasian Chair for Physics at Cambridge University. Dr. Ellen Klein taught philosophy at Flagler College in Florida and is now an independent scholar living in Washington DC.

"Space Exploration: Humanity's Single Most Important Moral Imperative," by E. R. Klein, 2007. Reprinted by permission.

As you read, consider the following questions:

1. What does the author use Easter Island to illustrate?
2. Does the author assign more value to human life or to planets?
3. Which 19th century scientist demonstrated that species evolve according to adaptive traits?

E veryone is familiar with the giant stone heads of Easter Island, a tiny and remote island in the South Eastern Pacific, about 1800 miles off the coast of Chile. Nearly a thousand of these huge statues, probably made for religious purposes, stand like sentries guarding a small patch of land that was not discovered by Europeans until 1722. Easter Island's first inhabitants probably arrived around 400 AD, and linguistic and genetic evidence suggested they most likely came from East Polynesia. It is estimated that the original landing party contained only about 100 people.

What makes Easter Island important to us, however, has nothing to do with how or why people migrated to this isolated spot, nor how they lived. Instead, what I am interested in is how and why this culture, known as the Rapanui, came to grief. It seems that due to their religious zeal (i.e., the creation and erection of the giant statues or Moai, which needed to be transported to their destinations via numerous logs), the Rapanui suffered a history of "deforestation, soil depletion, and erosion… an overall devastating ecological scenario resulting in overpopulation, food shortages, cannibalism, and war." (Dr. Jo Anne Van Tilburg, *Nova*, PBS Online, August 31, 2001.) Their complex culture imploded. With no trees left even to build fishing boats, the population shrank to a fifth of its previous level. That is, the Rapanui paid a huge price for "the way they chose to articulate their spiritual and political ideas." (ibid).

If the lesson from Easter Island is obvious, please forgive my forthcoming overstatement. People from all over the globe need to take seriously the likelihood that due to our various political and ideological ideas we too may be headed for disaster. In the wake of contemporary rainforest destruction; polluted oceans, rivers and lakes; holes in the ozone layer; food shortages due to floods, pestilence or drought; toxic waste, acid rain and nuclear fall-out (to name just a few environmental issues), humanity needs to realize that no amount of environmental policy can change the inevitable ecological scenario of the future—more people, less natural environment. From the First to the Third World, the future will contain billions more people who will need more and more food and resources while producing more and more waste. The picture is, simply, apocalypse soon.

All of this is just the consequences of reproduction. Add to this the persistent human desire to spread one's particular political agenda and/or religious ideals, and one quickly realizes that the planet Earth, even if it were kept ecologically tidy, is simply too small to give every group its own private, isolated, "holy" property. Under the reality of this "one planet island" scenario, September 11, 2001, was not just a day of mourning for the United States and her friends, but a day of warning to everyone on the globe.

The most pointed lesson from Easter Island is that if you live on an island where you continually deplete and pollute the resources, be sure to save something to escape on before it's too late. I imagine the surviving Rapanui, standing on the shore of Easter Island, now just a barren wasteland, saying, "We should probably have migrated somewhere else, or at least built an ark."

Space: The Only Real Frontier

Space, according to *Star Trek*, is the "final frontier." Given the above accounts of both human and planetary nature, it really is the only real frontier left.

In 1998, at the 44th Annual Meeting of the Florida Philosophical Association, Dr. Roy Weatherford gave his presidential address on the moral imperative of space travel. Weatherford argued that human lives are intrinsically valuable. This view, while controversial, is very widely held among philosophers. But Weatherford derived from this view a rather less commonly held conclusion. He said that if human beings are intrinsically valuable, then the more of them there are the better. Therefore, he reasoned, if we are to truly stand by our commitment to the value of human life, then not only is it immoral to argue for birth control, but, contrary to the belief of most philosophers, it is immoral to not argue in favor of maximum reproduction. That is, assuming that human life is of intrinsic value, then we all have a moral duty to create, recreate, and procreate human life as often, and in as many places, as we can. Given the obvious environmental constraints that are inherent to Earth, Weatherford then argued for an increase in funding for, and education about, space and space exploration, with a special emphasis on terraforming our Moon and Mars.

Though I don't share an immediate intuition that any and all human life is inherently or intrinsically valuable, the logic of his argument seems unassailable. If any and all human life is valuable for its own sake, then we have a duty to generate more of it (i.e., to reproduce), and we have this duty regardless of pollution, overcrowding and other environmental crises. Under such a moral imperative, humanity has no choice but to forge new frontiers for expansion. Space, with its nearly infinite possibilities for new places for human life to flourish, is the only real frontier left. This led Weatherford to conclude that it is humanity's number one global moral imperative to provide the educational and technological resources, as well as develop the overall mindset, for the advancement of space exploration and colonization.

Arguments Against Abandonment

Environmentalists from Aldo Leopold to Holmes Rolston III have argued that humans have a duty to broaden the scope of their moral framework and acknowledge that not only people have intrinsic moral value, but also animals, entire ecosystems, and ultimately the Earth itself. On this view, to treat the Earth and its resources solely as means to human ends is simply wrong. Those who believe that the Earth is itself intrinsically valuable may argue that it is therefore simply morally wrong to fly off and abandon our beautiful blue-green home.

Although the details of the numerous arguments for such a position are outside the scope of this article, let me offer a few comments and criticisms.

First, there is this pesky philosophical notion of value itself. From where is value bootstrapped? Most importantly for this discussion, how can one justify valuing the Earth without first having developed a relevant notion of value? Value simpliciter probably has its beginnings in the basic intuition that the "I" is valuable, and so anything relevantly similar to "I" is also valuable (i.e., other persons who act, look, etc., just like I do). The scope of value can be broadened from here, of course, via any number of analogous findings and connections, but not without the possible slippery pitfall into some kind of valuing everything on a par with everything else. My point here is not that a Buddhist-like "one equal with everything" view is wrong, but that such a view cannot easily be turned into any action at all, let alone specific actions toward "saving the Earth."

Even if one accepts that there are intrinsic values, and that people (for the most part) are the kinds of beings that have such value, the move toward valuing the Earth is not one small leap for mankind. After all, in most cases of value, at least the potential for reciprocity is a necessary, if not sufficient, condition for value. That is, one of the reasons that we value people is because people, by definition, have the potential to value—value themselves, value others, and, of course, to value valuing. When, for example, anti-abortionists argue their case, it is, at base because fetuses are at least potential, if not actual, people qua valuable and valuing beings. Or again, when animal rights activists argue their case, at bottom it is because animals (at whatever link on the evolutionary chain they draw the line) have demonstrated at least the potential, if not actual, ability to value—they attempt to avoid pain, they show affection for each other, show affection for humans, etc. But to extend the scope of value to the valuing of entire ecosystems, let alone the Earth as a whole, is a very problematic stretch indeed.

The Earth as Inherently Self-Destructive

This stretch is made even trickier by the history of the Earth itself. Even if one anthropomorphizes "her," the history of the Earth is one of a very inconsistent being, let alone in any way morally stable. If there are "laws of nature" which she supposedly follows, they are nothing less than cruel and unusual. Individuals of all species die all kinds of traumatic and painful deaths, and species themselves frequently go out of existence.

In what sense then does the Earth itself value any particular kind of moral (or even aesthetic, etc.) goals? And even if it were meaningful to talk about the Earth having interest in its own existence, what existence would it be proper to say is best for it? One as in the beginning, in which it was a hunk of molten rock? Or a later incarnation, as it cooled and allowed the life we now know as Jurassic? Can we say that the Earth is better off with more primeval forests than with sprawling industrial cities? With teaming diverse species, or just one huge lump of humanity? Maybe the Earth should be more like the Moon, pockmarked, barren, and silent? Or ultimately, maybe the Earth would prefer its inevitable state, of returning to the cosmic dust from whence it came? Which of all of these possible incarnations—past, present or future—is the most consistent with the Earth's proper function and destiny, or the one it ought to sustain? Such questions, even if meaningful, would certainly have no obvious answer which would be consistent with both the desires of the ecologist on the one hand and the human expansionist on the other. In fact, the values and valuing of any non-valuing being are nearly incomprehensible.

However, it is also a fact that humans use terms such as "value" to describe our normative intuitions and weigh our concerns with respect to even the most inanimate of objects, such as works of art—a form of valuing which is, again, dependent on valuing humanity. Why is this any less problematic than valuing the Earth? Perhaps most essentially because the Earth is not an artifact; that is, it is not a artful creation of our genius.

One could argue that the Earth, although not a human creation, does derive a great deal of value from its uniqueness, or what we believe is its uniqueness. After all, when there are hundreds of thousands of acres of Brazilian Rainforest it is not at all appalling, even from the perspective of the most hard-core environmentalist, to imagine justly allowing a certain portion of it to be set aside for deforestation in the name of the agricultural desires of the indigenous peoples. However, the last patch of American wilderness conducive to the sustaining of the now infamous Spotted Owl will not be so easily sacrificed. Scarcity is the issue relating to value here.

What then if there were dozens, thousands, no millions of other worlds at least as biodiverse and habitable as this one? What if the universe, in its nearly infinite hugeness, was simply packed with Earth-like M Class planets? How can the value of one planet ever override the value of spreading our humanity?

More Arguments for Colonizing Space

Regardless of where one stands on these issues of value, one can give other reasons to support space colonization.

First is what I call the fresh canvas argument. In the same way that a blank computer screen, blank piece of paper or, literally a blank canvas allows one to begin developing ideas in a totally unfettered way, this is true about the possibilities offered by space colonization as well. When you buy a used home you are constrained by the original structure to make do with the situation. Even if one is permitted to add on a room, this must be done with an eye to fitting with the previous structure. But begin with an empty plot of land and the possibilities for personal creativity are greatly enhanced. There will always be some constraints, of course, given the terrain and location of the land, but certainly they are minimized by not having to deal with a previously established floor plan.

I believe the same is true about societies, civilizations and governments. Unfortunately, even if the population of the planet never gained even one more person, there really is nowhere on Earth where the political soil is pristine enough to allow for new, maybe better, social/economic/political systems to take root and thrive. Given the present state of the world—with ancient religious hatreds, mega-corporations having global reach, and the internet—there is little room for a single family of hard-core frontiersmen, let alone any kind of new republic.

To be honest, the problem of space may exist even in space, at least for the possibly inhabitable spaces nearest Earth. Pluto, Uranus, Neptune, Saturn, Jupiter, Venus and Mercury are for various reasons unfeasible locations for human settlement. That leaves us with Mars, and of course the Moon, both of which are already tainted by politics and special interests. Even these off-world places, as well as their surrounding space, are already under the auspices of agencies such as the United Nations, with written documents of rules and regulations, such as the "Declaration of Legal Principles Governing the Activities of States in the Exploration and Use of Outer Space" and the "Status of International Agreements Relating to Activities in Outer Space." Maybe there really is no room for anything new "under the sun."

But if one sees the Moon, Mars, and the now mostly constructed International Space Station as baby steps toward the exploration of space on a grander scale, then in the long run such UN, etc., intervention will have little impact on human colonization and social experimentation. Furthermore, outer space is one of the few places where the governments of the world may actually work together toward specific goals.

This brings me to another reason for space exploration: the opportunity for our species to further evolve. In the mid 19th century Darwin demonstrated that species evolve in accordance with adaptive traits conducive to reproductive selection in particular ecosystems. That is, those individuals best adapted to their environment were able to breed adaptive traits into the next generation, etc. etc., until all the species evolved into the forms of life we see today. One of the main sources of empirical evidence used by Darwin in developing his theory of evolution were the finches of the small Galapagos Islands. For example, the finches imprisoned on one of the islands drink the nectar of flowers which cover the island. Another species, however, marooned on a different tiny island with no vegetation or bugs, has survived by adapting to drinking the blood of the Galapagos Lizards that bask daily in the sun in order to "stomach cook" the underwater vegetation they themselves have adapted to feed on. These island-specific finch populations evolved from a single species. They show that harsh and odd circumstances force evolutionary change to take place.

The questions that come to the fore for us now are: Has human evolution reached its pinnacle? Are we stagnating as a species? Is it true that until the actual physiology of our brains changes again, similar to the degree and kind of change our evolutionary ancestors went through from Homo erectus to Homo sapiens, we will see only modest progress for humanity? Furthermore, is it the case that the Earth no longer holds any environment that we cannot alter to fit the state of development we've already achieved? And finally, aren't the virtually infinite number of strange, unforeseeable, and unyielding environments in outer space and on other planets precisely what humanity needs to evolve into its next stage?

Conclusions

These arguments are not to say that I think it is irrational to work toward global peace, overall environmental health, and an end to famine and serious epidemics. Such goals are important, but maybe they should be put into a more "universal" perspective, valued more instrumentally, for maintaining a relatively stable world which will finally allow humanity to work toward our mastery of outer space. If we are to truly achieve our potential, and not have human history end here on Earth, regardless of how healthily, peacefully, and contentedly—let alone slip away like the Rapanui of Easter Island—then we require a commitment of extra-global proportions. Only the limits of the universe itself should limit humanity's dreams.

Update: Hawking Backs Space Exploration

Dr. Klein's article was originally sent to *Philosophy Now* in 2003. Since June 2006, the renowned British astrophysicist Stephen Hawking has also begun to make statements supporting large-scale colonization of space. In a lecture in Hong Kong, he said that "Life on Earth is at the ever-increasing risk of being wiped out by a disaster, such as sudden global warming, nuclear war, a genetically engineered virus or other dangers we have not yet thought of... I think the human race has no future if it doesn't go into space." Hawking believes that in 100 years, there could be self-sufficient settlements in space.

In a personal bid to show the feasibility of mass space travel, Hawking, who is paralysed with Lou Gehrig's disease, successfully took a "zero gravity" flight in April this year (see picture). He says this is a step towards later taking a sub-orbital space journey. Richard Branson has offered to provide such a flight for Hawking in the next few years.

> *"New wealth in an innovation-driven economy requires the discovery and development of new ideas to solve old problems; the seizing of new opportunities with technology and ingenuity."*

Government Investment in Innovation Is Essential to Economic Growth

Jennifer Erickson and Sean Pool

In the following viewpoint—written in 2012, when the US government was facing automatic budget cuts, known as sequestration, that would reduce spending on a variety of government programs in order to reduce the government's deficit—Jennifer Erickson and Sean Pool explain the value of government investment innovation. They go on to discuss several specific programs, including the space program, that have provided an excellent return on that investment. The authors close with a powerful call for continued government investment in science and research. Erickson has served as the assistant director of innovation and growth at the White House Office of Science and Technology policy. Pool works in the finance industry at the intersection of energy, technology, and environment.

This material ["The High Return on Investment for Publicly Funded Research," by Jennifer Erickson and Sean Pool, December 10, 2012] was first published by Science Progress (www.scienceprogress.org). Reprinted with permission of the Center for American Progress.

As you read, consider the following questions:

1. According to the viewpoint, how does investment in innovative fields, such as space exploration, help create wealth?
2. Why do you think President John F. Kennedy was willing to risk such a large investment in the space program?
3. What are some of the most exciting innovations mentioned by the authors? Were you surprised to learn they were the result of government research projects?

I nvesting in innovation pays off.

The World Economic Forum, an international non-governmental organization that assesses global business and socioeconomic policy, classified the United States in the 21st century as an "innovation-driven economy." This means that the creation of new wealth depends not just on traditional inputs like natural resources, land, or labor—or on increasing the efficiency of existing capabilities. Rather, new wealth in an innovation-driven economy requires the discovery and development of new ideas to solve old problems; the seizing of new opportunities with technology and ingenuity.

But the importance of innovation is not measured simply in new inventions. Innovation also requires dissemination through market adoption and public acceptance. While the private sector has a key role to play in making innovation happen, government must provide three key public-good inputs that allow innovation to blossom: investments in human capital, infrastructure, and research.

January will bring deep budget cuts to all three of these critical innovation investments if President Barack Obama and Washington lawmakers don't avert the automatic spending cuts in the so-called fiscal showdown debate over how to reduce the deficit.

To be sure, deficit reduction is an important national priority, but as President Obama said in 2011, "Cutting the deficit by gutting our investments in innovation and education is like lightening an overloaded airplane by removing its engine. It may make you feel like you're flying high at first, but it won't take long before you feel the impact."

The Center for American Progress has previously highlighted how investments in all three areas are critical to our competitiveness. Today we'll take a closer look at one of these key innovation ingredients: research.

Government Research Provides a High Return on Investment

To continue leading the world in innovation and welcoming the businesses and industries of the future, the United States must continue its long history of robust investments in research and development in the increasingly interconnected fields of physical sciences, computational sciences, life sciences, social sciences, and engineering.

The value of these investments is borne out by history. According to economists Charles Jones and John Williams of Stanford University, the National Bureau of Economic Research, and the Federal Reserve Bank of San Francisco, the return on investment for publicly funded scientific research and development is somewhere between 30 percent and 100 percent, or more.

Consider just a few of the breakthrough innovations that have stemmed from government investments in research:

Department of Energy Labs: 1943–Present
Founded in 1943 to address the need to mobilize our nation's scientific assets to support the war effort—including the Manhattan Project and development of radar—and then afterward to consolidate and repurpose our national investments in military research.

What we invested: A few million dollars in the early 1940s, growing to about $5 billion, or 0.03 percent of GDP, in 2012. (Note: The Department of Energy labs also receive funding from other government agencies outside the department, bringing the total spending of the system closer to $10 billion.)

What we got: The optical digital recording technology behind all music, video, and data storage; fluorescent lights; communications and observation satellites; advanced batteries now used in electric cars; modern water-purification techniques that make drinking water safe for millions; supercomputers used by government, industry, and consumers every day; more resilient passenger jets; better cancer therapies; and the confirmation that it was an asteroid that killed the dinosaurs 65 million years ago.

National Science Foundation: 1950–Present

Championed by Sen. Harley Kilgore of West Virginia, a New Deal politician and small-business man with a deep distrust of the laissez-faire attitude toward science and of large monopolies that at the time controlled much of the country's scientific enterprise. In response to these issues, the National Science Foundation was founded "to promote the progress of science; to advance the national health, prosperity, and welfare; and to secure the national defense."

What we invested: Just $3.5 million for its first full year of operation in 1952 (roughly $29 million in 2012 dollars), growing to $7 billion, or 0.05 percent of GDP, in 2012.

What we got: Google, which was started by a couple of students working on a research project supported by the National Science Foundation, is today worth an estimated $250 billion and employs 54,000 people. This alone would pay for nearly all the program's costs reaching back to its inception, but funding has also been instrumental in the development of new technologies and companies in nearly every major industry, including advanced electronics, computing, digital communications, environmental resource management, lasers, advanced manufacturing, clean energy, nanotechnology, biotechnology, and higher education.

Defense Advanced Research Projects Agency, or DARPA: 1958–Present

Founded in response to the launch of Sputnik to ensure the United States had cutting-edge military technology, the Defense Advanced Research Projects Agency now operates as a small R&D team within the Department of Defense, delivering world-leading technology both on the battlefield (think stealth fighter jets) and off (think the Internet). Describing itself today as "one hundred geniuses connected by a travel agent," the agency continues to work with universities and teams across the country to push scientific boundaries, working on projects like a human exoskeleton and mobile robots capable of performing medical operations.

What we invested: $246 million in the first appropriation in 1962. In 2011 dollars: $1.6 billion. Investment has continued, reaching nearly $3 billion, or 0.02 percent of GDP, in 2012.

What we got: The team that would go on to pioneer technologies that brought us the Internet, the Global Positioning System, and Siri.

The Apollo Space Program: 1961–1969

Two months after the Soviet Union put the first man in orbit, President John F. Kennedy announced the Apollo Space Program to a joint session of Congress, telling the nation, "No single space project in this period will be more impressive to mankind, or more important in the long-range exploration of space; and none will be so difficult or expensive to accomplish." He was right. In fixing a national ambition and rallying resources behind it, the United States went from never having put a man in orbit to landing a team on the moon in less than a decade. At the height of Apollo's efforts, it employed 400,000 Americans and worked with 20,000 partnering institutions.

What we invested: $24 billion. In 2011 dollars: $150 billion.

What we got: Massive technological advancement and the start of huge opportunities for technology transfer, leading to more than 1,500 successful spinoffs related to areas as disparate as heart monitors, solar panels, and cordless innovation. More recently, we've seen a fledgling private-sector American space industry with real growth potential, which in 2012 completed its first cargo delivery to the International Space Station.

Human Genome Project: 1988–2003

Started as a joint project between the Department of Energy and the National Institutes of Health, the Human Genome Project ultimately helped coordinate the work of scientists in countries around the world to map the human genome. In a joint telecast in 2000, President Bill Clinton and U.K. Prime Minister Tony Blair announced the first phase was complete, with a public working draft of the "genetic blueprint for human beings," ushering in a new era of medical and scientific advancement.

What we invested: $3.6 billion, or approximately 0.005 percent of GDP spread out over 15 years. In 2011 dollars: roughly $5.7 billion in total.

What we got: Critical tools to help identify, treat, and prevent causes of disease—and huge opportunities for the high-growth American biotechnology industry, which accounts for more than three-quarters of $1 trillion in economic output, or 5.4 percent of GDP, in 2010, and now depends heavily on these advances in genetics.

The Future of Federally Funded Research

While we have seen huge and tangible results from our research investments in the past, we are not making the level of investments we need to cultivate innovation in the 21st century. Our national investments in research and development as a percentage of discretionary public spending have fallen from a 17 percent high at the height of the space race in 1962 to about 9 percent today, reflecting a shift in priorities of our government. The biggest decline has taken place in civilian research and development, which has dropped significantly as a proportion of both GDP and federal spending.

To make matters worse, the automatic budget cuts set to take effect January 1, 2012, would reduce research and development budgets by 8.4 percent on average. And independent analysis by the Aerospace Industries Association predicted that these cuts would put 31,000 physical, life, and social scientists across the country out of work, and reduce the success rate of science research grant applications at the National Science Foundation and National Institutes of Health from an average of about one-in-five to one-in-six.

To ensure that the United States remains a leader in the 21st-century innovation economy, we need to double down on our investments in technology, the enabler of long-term efficiency gains and economic growth, and also change the way we think about the converging fields of science, technology, and business. Specifically, we must:

- Avert severe cuts to US science research that would take effect under sequestration, and put key science agencies—such as the National Science Foundation, the Energy Department's Office of Science, and the National Institute of Standards and Technology—on a path that will see their budgets double by the end of the decade or sooner, like we did for the National Institutes of Health in the past decade

- Think more holistically about our national innovation ecosystem by taking steps to help universities and national laboratories—the two biggest performers of federally funded research—and engage with industry to help get good ideas out of the lab and into the market faster

- Reform our government systems to streamline the grant-making processes for technology, engineering, small business, and community- and region-based economic and workforce-development programs that support clusters of innovation and talent across the country

Conclusion

At a time when economic success in the global market is determined more than ever by the pace of innovation, we cannot afford to reduce our investments in research. As the president said in his State of the Union speech last year, "In America, innovation doesn't just change our lives, it's how we make our living." While innovation may be in our national DNA, we can't take it for granted.

VIEWPOINT

> *"Space exploration began over
> 40 years ago, yet only three countries
> —and China's case is as yet unproven
> —appear to have the capability to
> put humans in space. And none has
> been able to promote space visits on a
> sustainable, commercial scale."*

Space Tourism Might Not Get Off the Ground
David B. Sawaya

*Until now, space exploration has been left to the professionals,
exceptionally well-trained astronauts who have "the right stuff."
But now we are entering the age of space tourism, where anyone in
decent health and with enough money has a shot at walking among
the stars. In the following viewpoint, David B. Sawaya argues that
there are considerable dangers of commercial space exploration.
The author explores the practical considerations of space tourism,
particularly regarding its potential for catastrophe. Sawaya is an
engineer and policy analyst for the Organisation for Economic
Cooperation and Development.*

David B. Sawaya, "Space Tourism: Is It safe?" ©OECD Observer No 242, March 2004.
http://oecdobserver.org/news/archivestory.php/aid/1242/Space_tourism:_Is_it_safe_.html

As you read, consider the following questions:

1. Why does the author say that space tourism is potentially more dangerous than extreme sports?
2. What three issues does the author list as being the real problems for a space tourism industry?
3. What more realistic possibilities might result from space technology according to the viewpoint?

The space age may be entering a new phase, but the issue of safety continues to weigh against ambitious ideas about manned travel in large numbers, particularly tourism.

"We do not know where this journey will end, yet we know this: human beings are headed into the cosmos." With these words, the US president, George W. Bush, launched in January his ambitious vision for a new US programme for human space exploration. A new manned spaceship for a trip to the moon by 2015, not just to visit but to spend time there, would open the way for manned missions "to worlds beyond," including to Mars.

The president's announcement followed hot on the heels of one from the Russian Space Agency (Rosaviacosmos), that it was planning to send two civilian "space tourists" and a professional cosmonaut to the International Space Station aboard a Russian Soyuz rocket in 2005. Moreover, the Soyuz trip will be the first privately funded manned space launch ever.

Space enthusiasts are delighted at this flurry of renewed interest, and the fact that China has succeeded in sending a person into orbit merely heightens the stakes and intensifies the competition. Even the Europeans are locking heads and planning a strategy to get to Mars in the coming half-century.

But to see in these initiatives the dawn of a space tourism age would be making a leap of faith. True, space's return to the top of the international policy agenda has to be welcomed, not least for its commercial potential (see box). On the other hand, why has it taken so long? Space exploration began over 40 years ago, yet only three countries—and China's case is as yet unproven—appear to have the capability to put humans in space. And none has been able to promote space visits on a sustainable, commercial scale.

The US programme intends to tackle this, though we must be realistic. The budget announced to get the programme off the ground will be high. According to the White House, most of the funding needed for the new programme will come from reallocating US$11 billion of NASA's current five-year budget of US$86 billion, and adding another billion dollars over five years. While some commentators say this will not be enough, expense is only one problem to consider. The real tricky issue is safety.

The tragic break up of the space shuttle Columbia on 1 February 2003 was a reminder of how dangerous space travel still is, despite 40 years of development. In fact, space travel is much more dangerous than any other form of transportation, including driving a car. In the US manned space programme, there have been 17 fatalities in 732 person flights. That means an astonishing 2,320 deaths per 100,000 passengers, which is 45,000 times more dangerous than flying in a commercial airplane. Put another way, two space shuttles have crashed in 113 departures, which is a 1.8% failure rate. This would be unacceptable for commercial airplanes, which see an average of about 0.4 accidents per 100,000 departures per year in the US.

In other words, space travel, while desirable, is just too hazardous to become a major tourist activity. It is even more dangerous than so-called "extreme" sports, such as scuba diving or sky diving.

Russia has had a better success rate. In fact, it has not had a manned vehicle failure board its Soyuz rocket since 1971. This is a result of the Russian tendency to build simple systems using reliable "off-the-shelf" components, which, together with low labour costs, contribute to producing one of the cheapest launchers on the market.

Cheap is a relative term, however; the price of an unmanned Soyuz is approximately US$35 million, while a manned vehicle costs much more as a result of the complex life support and atmospheric re-entry systems. How can one of the cheapest launch vehicles in the world still be so prohibitively expensive?

The main problem with the Soyuz is that none of it is reusable; even the small passenger capsule that returns to Earth is not reused. Most experts agree that a truly increased human presence in space will only be achieved by combining total or near-total reusability with a quick turnaround time and easy inspectability. In the late 1960s, after its successful moon missions, NASA began to focus on creating a reusable launch vehicle (RLV) that would drastically reduce the cost of space travel. This goal, which manifested itself in the creation of the Space Shuttle, has not been reached. Ironically, the Space Shuttle is the most expensive launch vehicle in the world (estimates range from US$350 to US$500 million per flight), even though it has reusable parts.

Why does the Space Shuttle cost so much? For a start, it requires a veritable army of ground personnel to inspect the vehicle after each flight and prepare it for the next one. It is only reusable after the vehicle has essentially been taken apart and reassembled. The thermal protection system alone takes 30,000 people-hours (3,750 working days) to inspect, refurbish and reinstall between flights. This labour intensive process is one reason why the US space shuttle fleet has never flown more than nine times in any one year. This is far too few flights for a large tourism market.

Assuming there is a demand, just how big (or small) might that tourism market be? First of all, manned space flight is beyond the pockets of most ordinary people. There have been two space tourists, both multimillionaires, reportedly paying some US$20 million to fly aboard the Russian Soyuz rocket and spend 10 days aboard the International Space Station. There are not very many people in the world who are capable of paying this much. In fact, the market would only be about 100,000 people. And then, only a small percentage—experts say about 1%—of that number would be willing to pay for a space flight.

Launch costs have remained essentially stagnant since the beginning of space flight in the late 1950s, but what would the market result be if ticket prices dropped to US$1 million per launch into orbit? At this price, the market is much larger and using the same assumptions as above, there would be approximately 72,500 paying participants. A lot, but certainly not enough for a mass revolution. Not everyone shares this scepticism. Take the X Prize foundation, which is seen by many as the bellwether of space tourism. The foundation will award US$10 million to the first team which builds a vehicle capable of taking three passengers to a suborbital altitude of 100 km and repeating the feat within a week. Perhaps this more open, competitive, model could achieve progress at a fraction of current costs. Indeed, some speculate that such ventures could open the way to sub-orbital joyrides at around US$100,000 a ticket. But there are obvious dangers, not least of which is the risk of corner cutting on safety to make that fast turnaround and ultimately running the risk of another disaster.

Cosmic Cocktail

The real problem facing space tourism is not any one of the issues described above. Rather, it is all of them blended together: cost, safety and market-size. The more safety ingredients you add to the cocktail, like back-up systems or escape options, the more expensive it becomes. In fact, due to the additional complexity of the overall system, some argue that increasing spacecraft reliability from 96% to 99% would be as expensive as the reliability increase from 80% to 96%. This leaves space tourism entrepreneurs with a bit of a chicken and egg problem: how to realise affordable launches that are safe at the same time.

There are a number of steps that government and private space capitalists could take, though. First, they should stop thinking of space as a place for tourism, at least initially. The focus should be on other commercial endeavours, with tourism developing as a bonus. After all, in the automobile, railway and aviation industries, commercial needs drove mass production and cost reduction, which eventually paved the way for tourism.

And there are plenty of commercial incentives for going into space, in particular the prospect of harnessing valuable resources, like Helium-3 on the moon, as well as the engineering and technical spinoffs of the R&D needed to get there. The possible discovery of water on Mars could pave the way for human exploration and eventual exploitation, since with water we can produce oxygen needed to breathe and hydrogen for rocket fuel.

Second, technology must of course be improved, so that spacecraft are developed with the same safety and reliability characteristics as today's commercial airplanes. Research is going on throughout the world, but funding is low and much of the technology being developed is just an evolution of what is commonplace now. More effort may be needed to make the breakthrough that could be revolutionary. However, with NASA already having to cut the budget for the Next Generation Launch Technology program to fund the agency's new exploration programme, it remains to be seen whether the funding to make such a breakthrough will be there.

Finally, spacecraft design procedures must be changed so that inspectability and turnaround time requirements are satisfied. Also, modifications to allow some in-flight repair should be considered. Ideally, a spacecraft should be designed with parts that can easily and quickly be changed. Without this, a substantial tourism market might not get off the ground simply because vehicles will be unable to fly frequently enough. Nor would investing in a much bigger airline-type fleet be an automatic solution, since inspection times would still be long and costs too high.

With all the difficulties of space travel, why are private investors so interested in the commercial prospects of space, especially given the notoriously high development costs and reputation for time overruns and failures? A need to expand may be the simple answer, and government support in partnership with private entrepreneurs may one day bring space's full commercial potential within reach of holidaymakers.

Until then, there may be more modest opportunities on the horizon. Take the US Department of Defense's Falcon programme to develop a hypersonic bomber by the year 2025. This would have considerable spin-off potential. Coast-to-coast travel in the US would take 30 minutes, while Sydney would be just over an hour away from Paris and London. The vehicles developed in the Falcon programme could be modified to travel through the upper reaches of the atmosphere and allow people to experience weightlessness from microgravity, while getting from A to B. Hypersonic planes will cut travel times by 90%, not just the 50% allowed by the recently decommissioned Concorde. Also, hypersonic planes will have better fuel efficiency for a wider global reach, and by flying at twice the height of Concorde, they will emit less of the noise pollution that was such a major obstacle to Concorde's expansion.

Floating around on a hypersonic plane might not sound as exciting a prospect as heading away into outer space. But cost and safety mean that, while space exploration must continue, for the general public, the sky will probably be the limit for a while yet.

> *"The challenges of space exploration have sparked new scientific and technological knowledge of inherent value to humankind, leading to better understanding of our Universe and the solar system in which we live."*

Space Exploration Is a Good Investment

NASA

At the end of the previous viewpoint, the author suggested a few possible—what he called "more modest"—opportunities that might result from the current generation of space technology. In the following viewpoint (excerpted for length), authors from NASA highlight some of the benefits of space research. The authors use historical information, going back to the first satellites, to make their case. The benefits of space exploration, both practical and economic, are many and varied—and often surprising. National Aeronautics and Space Administration (NASA) is an agency of the US government that oversees the space program and space research.

"Benefits Stemming from Space Exploration", NASA, September 2013.

As you read, consider the following questions:

1. What societal benefits does this report list as having come directly from the space program?
2. How, according to this viewpoint, does space exploration and the associated research benefit humans culturally?
3. Does this viewpoint make a strong case that continued space exploration is a good investment?

More than fifty years of human activity in space have produced societal benefits that improve the quality of life on Earth. The first satellites, designed to study the space environment and test initial capabilities in Earth orbit, contributed critical knowledge and capabilities for developing satellite telecommunications, global positioning, and advances in weather forecasting. Space exploration initiated the economic development of space that today, year after year, delivers high returns for invested funds in space[1]. The challenges of space exploration have sparked new scientific and technological knowledge of inherent value to humankind, leading to better understanding of our Universe and the solar system in which we live. Knowledge, coupled with ingenuity, provides people around the globe with solutions as well as useful products and services. Knowledge acquired from space exploration has also introduced new perspectives on our individual and collective place in the Universe.

Future space exploration goals call for sending humans and robots beyond Low Earth Orbit and establishing sustained access to destinations such as the Moon, asteroids and Mars. Space agencies participating in the International Space Exploration Coordination Group (ISECG)[2] are discussing an international approach for achieving these goals, documented in ISECG's Global Exploration Roadmap[3]. That approach begins with the International Space Station (ISS), and leads to human missions to the surface of Mars.

Employing the complementary capabilities of both humans and robotic systems will enable humankind to meet this most ambitious

Sending More Humans into Space Could Help Those Back Home

Research dating back to the early years of the space race has led to technologies that benefit us all. Many scientific discoveries have come since the arrival of inhabitable space stations that act as orbital laboratories. NASA's first space station Skylab helped understand the effects on the human body of spending months in space and paved the way for the International Space Station.

A huge number of research studies have been completed on the ISS since the year 2000 in the areas of human physiology, biology, biotechnology, physical science and earth and space science. These studies have led to discoveries such as enhanced protein crystal growth for drug development, efficient combustion of fuel droplets, and an understanding of the effects of long duration exposure to microgravity on the human body, revealing that spaceflight has effects similar to ageing on Earth.

Despite much human physiological research being carried out in space, it has one major limitation – there are simply not enough humans currently going to space to act as research participants, leading to difficulties in research design. In fact, only 550 or so humans have ever been into space since Russian cosmonaut Yuri Gagarin first orbited the Earth in 1961.

space exploration challenge, and to increase benefits for society. These benefits can be categorized into three fundamental areas: innovation; culture and inspiration; and new means to address global challenges.

Innovation. There are numerous cases of societal benefits linked to new knowledge and technology from space exploration. Space exploration has contributed to many diverse aspects of everyday life, from solar panels to implantable heart monitors, from cancer therapy to light-weight materials, and from water-purification systems to improved computing systems and to a global search-and-rescue system[4]. [...] Space exploration will continue to be an essential driver for opening up new domains

Human physiological experiments in space tend to have very small participant numbers (for example, the NASA twins study) or they have to take place over many years. Could the boom in commercial human spaceflight accelerate the speed of human physiological discoveries in space? We certainly think so.

Commercial spaceflight companies such as SpaceX and Orbital are already launching rockets taking supplies and research equipment to the International Space Station. SpaceX is developing its habitable Dragon capsule to take space tourists around the moon, with ambitions to use its sibling, Red Dragon, to land astronauts on Mars.

Others are developing sub-orbital spaceplanes, such as Virgin Galactic's SpaceShipTwo, which will enable passengers to experience microgravity for a number of minutes or travel 30 times faster between cities than passenger airlines. To safely send throngs of space tourists beyond the atmosphere, we need to understand the health implications of just getting these "non-professional" astronauts into space through new medical research, and developing spaceports will provide access to exciting new platforms to expand these frontiers of science.

"Space Tourism Could Help Boost Science and Health Research – Here's How", by Nick Caplan, Andrew Winnard and Kirsty Lindsay, The Conversation, June 22, 2017.

in science and technology, triggering other sectors to partner with the space sector for joint research and development. This will return immediate benefits back to Earth in areas such as materials, power generation and energy storage, recycling and waste management, advanced robotics, health and medicine, transportation, engineering, computing and software. Furthermore, innovations required for space exploration, such as those related to miniaturisation, will drive improvements in other space systems and services resulting in higher performance and lower cost. These will in turn result in better services on Earth and better return of investment in institutional and commercial space activities. In addition, the excitement generated by space exploration attracts young people to careers in science, technology, engineering and mathematics, helping to build global capacity for scientific and technological innovation.

Culture and Inspiration. Space exploration offers a unique and evolving perspective on humanity's place in the Universe, which is common to all. Every day, space exploration missions fulfill people's curiosity, producing fresh data about the solar system that brings us closer to answering profound questions that have been asked for millennia: What is the nature of the Universe? Is the destiny of humankind bound to Earth? Are we and our planet unique? Is there life elsewhere in the Universe?

New Means to Address Global Challenges. Partnerships and capabilities developed through space exploration create new opportunities for addressing global challenges. Space exploration is a global endeavour contributing to trust and diplomacy between nations. Enhanced global partnerships and exploration capabilities may help advance international preparedness for protecting the Earth from catastrophic events such as some asteroid strikes, advancing collaborative research on space weather and protecting spacecraft by developing new means for space debris removal. Knowledge derived from space exploration may also contribute to implementing policies for environmentally sustainable development.

In summary, space scientists and engineers who overcame past challenges could not have predicted all the ways in which their innovations are now being used on Earth. Though the precise nature of future benefits from space exploration is unpredictable, current trends suggest that significant benefits may be generated in areas such as new materials, health and medicine, transportation, and computer technology. New opportunities for job creation and economic growth are being created by private enterprises that are increasingly investing in space exploration and seeking ways to make space exploration more affordable and reliable, and thus, more sustainable and profitable.

There is no activity on Earth that matches the unique challenges of space exploration. The first fifty years of space activity have generated benefits for people around the globe. This past record gives strong reason for confidence that renewed investments in space exploration will have similarly positive impacts for future generations.

[...]

Notes

1. OECD Handbook on Measuring the Space Economy, March 2012.

2. ISECG space agencies include, in alphabetical order: ASI (Italy), CNES (France), CNSA (China), CSA (Canada), CSIRO (Australia), DLR (Germany), ESA (Europe), ISRO (India), JAXA (Japan), KARI (Republic of Korea), NASA (United States of America), NSAU (Ukraine), Roscosmos (Russia), UKSA (United Kingdom).

3. The Global Exploration Roadmap can be downloaded at www.globalspaceexploration .org.

4. Spinoff materials published by the National Aeronautics and Space Administration (e.g. Spinoff database, spinoff.nasa.gov/spinoff/database; Spinoff 2012, spinoff.nasa.gov /Spinoff2012).

> "Private companies are vying for
> a slice of the Moon pie, lured
> by Google's multi-million dollar
> XPRIZE that challenges entrants to
> develop low-cost methods for robotic
> space exploration."

The Moon Is Suddenly Prime Real Estate

Marc Norman and Penelope King

In 1969 the Moon was a mysterious frontier. Soon it may be a rest stop. In the following viewpoint Marc Norman and Penelope King argue that many countries—most of which are new to the space race— are gearing up for Moon landings. The motivations are complex, say the authors, but most often come down to the missions' benefits to countries and companies on Earth, much like we saw in the previous viewpoint. Norman is deputy director of the Australian affiliate of the NASA Solar System Exploration Virtual institute (SSERVI). King is associate professor at Australian National University.

"Five Reasons India, China and Other Nations Plan to Travel to the Moon," by Marc Norman and Penelope King, The Conversation, November 20, 2017. https:// theconversation.com/five-reasons-india-china-and-other-nations-plan-to-travel-to-the-moon-87589. Licensed Under CC BY-ND 4.0 International.

As you read, consider the following questions:

1. According to the viewpoint, nations with no history of space exploration are beginning to get into the space race 2.0. Why are they doing this now?
2. Why might countries want to stake a claim on the Moon, and why now, according to the viewpoint?
3. How have advances in robotics changed the game when it comes to space exploration?

N o human has been to the Moon since 1972 and only 12 people have ever done it—all of them American men.

But that list could soon be getting a lot longer.

Why the Moon? Haven't we already been there, done that? Well, yes. But now there are new reasons motivating countries to reach the Moon.

Human and other missions to the Moon are planned by India, China and Russia, as well as Japan and Europe. South Korea and North Korea are also looking towards the Moon.

Even NASA seems to be getting its mojo back, recently announcing a revamped vision for a Deep Space Gateway that includes a port of call at the Moon en route to Mars and beyond. Elon Musk has also called for a Moon base.

Private companies are vying for a slice of the Moon pie, lured by Google's multi-million dollar XPRIZE that challenges entrants to develop low-cost methods for robotic space exploration.

A space race of sorts seems to back on in earnest, for five reasons.

Reason 1: A Vision for Innovation

In the past and still now, one reason that space attracts interest and investment is that humans seem driven to explore and push the limits, physically and viscerally.

But space also acts as a unifying force, providing a clear vision that pushes technology and innovation forwards.

After several decades of relative neglect, space exploration is again seen as driving technology, inspiring engagement with science and engineering, and creating national pride. The program at the recent International Astronautical Congress in Adelaide captured that sentiment.

These motivators are seen as especially important by emerging economies like India, China and Russia, which means that more established players like Europe and the USA have to work harder keep up.

The recent announcement that Australia will have a space agency is expected to create new opportunities for this country.

Reason 2: Economic and Geopolitical Advantages

Paradoxically, exploration of the Moon builds both international cooperation and competition.

Even if they don't have their own space program, countries can develop instruments to fly on spacecraft that are built and launched by other nations. For example, India's Chandrayaan-1 spacecraft carried instruments from Sweden, Germany, UK, Bulgaria, and the US to the Moon. This helps mesh economies and provides strong motivation to keep the peace.

Economic and geopolitical competition occurs because the Moon is seen as unclaimed territory. No country is allowed to own the Moon, at least according to a 1967 UN Treaty that has agreement from over 100 countries.

Nonetheless, there are incentives to place a claim on the Moon. For example, helium-3 (an isotope of the element helium) is abundant on the Moon, but rare on Earth. It is a potential fuel for nuclear fusion, a potentially unlimited and non-polluting source of energy. China, in particular, has stated a strong interest in lunar helium-3.

The situation appears similar to that of Antarctica in the 1950s, when the continent was subdivided by the 12 countries that had active scientific programs in the region at the time. Sending a spacecraft to the Moon—even if it fails prematurely like India's Chandrayaan-1—may provide a compelling case for recognition if the Moon were ever to be carved up into zones of research and economic development.

Russia, China, Japan, Europe and the USA landed (or crashed) spacecraft on the Moon in the decades after Apollo.

Reason 3: An Easy Target

Growing space agencies need successful missions, and the Moon is a tempting target. Radio communication over the relatively short distance between the Earth and Moon (384,400 km) is almost instantaneous (1-2 sec). Between Earth and Mars, two-way communication times can be the better part of an hour.

The low gravity and lack of an atmosphere on the Moon also simplifies operations for orbiters and landers.

The Russian Luna missions showed that it is technically feasible to apply robotics to bring samples from the Moon to Earth. China aims to launch a robotic mission to the Moon in the next 1-2 years to fetch samples. If successful, these will be the first samples brought back from the Moon since Luna 24 in 1976.

Reason 4: New Discoveries

Despite decades of observations, each new mission to the Moon produces new discoveries.

Japan's Selene spacecraft and India's Chandrayaan-1 mission discovered new distributions of minerals on the Moon, and probed regions of potential resources.

An exciting discovery has been the presence of water ice and other organic compounds in permanently shadowed regions of the Moon that never see sunlight. If present in sufficient quantities, water ice on the Moon could be used as a resource for generating fuel or supporting human habitation. This would be a major advantage for future missions considering the cost of carrying water from the Earth to the Moon.

Although immense engineering advances are needed to recover these resources from environments as cold as -250°C, such challenges drive new technologies.

Reason 5: We Learn About Earth

Aside from the practicalities, exploration of the Moon has revealed completely new ideas about the origin of the solar system.

Prior to the Apollo missions, planets were thought to form over long periods of time by the slow agglomeration of dusty particles. Moon rocks returned to Earth by the Apollo missions changed that idea literally overnight. We now know that gigantic collisions between planets were common, and one such collision of a Mars-size planet with the Earth probably formed the Moon (animation).

We've also learned that the dark circular features on the Moon are scars of impacting asteroids stirred up by shifts in the orbits of Jupiter and Saturn.

Future studies of the Moon will undoubtedly lead to even deeper insights into the origin of the Earth, our home planet.

Space exploration is not only about "out there". Travel to the Moon creates jobs, technical innovations and new discoveries that improve the lives of all of us "down here".

Periodical and Internet Sources Bibliography

The following articles have been selected to supplement the diverse views presented in this chapter.

Anjana Ahuja, "The Global Technopolitics of Space Exploration, *Financial Times*, February 9, 2018. https://www.ft.com /content/68ee09e8-0ced-11e8-bacb-2958fde95e5e.

Justin Calderon, "The Tiny Nation Leading a New Space Race," BBC, 16 July 2018. http://www.bbc.com/future/story/20180716-the -tiny-nation-leading-a-new-space-race.

Kurt Eichenwald, "The Dirty Secrets Behind the Race to Put a Man on the Moon," *Newsweek*, September 17, 2014. https://www .newsweek.com/2014/09/26/dirty-secrets-behind-race-put-man -moon-271158.html.

Sandra Erwin, "Pentagon Report: China's Space Program 'Continues to Mature Rapidly," *Space News*, August 20, 2018. https:// spacenews.com/pentagon-report-chinas-space-program -continues-to-mature-rapidly.

Chabeli Hererra, "Never Been Busier: New Space Race Fuels Massive Economic Comeback on Space Coast," *The Orlando Sentinel*, September 4, 2018. https://www.orlandosentinel.com/business /os-brevard-county-space-economy-20180829-story.html.

Michael Kernan, "The Space Race: Onetime Rivals Are Now Partners," *Smithsonian*, 1997. https://www.smithsonianmag.com /history/the-space-race-141404095.

Earle Kyle, "Space Exploration Is Still the Brightest Hope-Bringer We Have," *Aeon*, 19 May 2017. https://aeon.co/ideas/one -extraordinary-scientist-and-the-story-of-space.

Elton Lossner, "The New Space Race," *Harvard Political Review*, May 26, 2017. http://harvardpolitics.com/covers/the-new-space-race.

George Musser, "Space Exploration Sticker Shock—Economics at NASA: The Laws of Physics Are Easy; It's Economics that Vexes NASA," *Scientific American*, January 1, 2009. https://www .scientificamerican.com/article/space-exploration-sticker-shock.

NASA, "15 Ways the International Space Staton is Benefitting Earth," NASA.com, October 30, 2015. https://www.nasa.gov/mission_pages/station/research/news/15_ways_iss_benefits_earth.

Carolyn Collins Petersen, "A Short History of Roscosmos and the Soviet Space Program, *ThoughtCo.*, updated January 17, 2018. https://www.thoughtco.com/soviet-space-program-history-4140631.

OPPOSING
VIEWPOINTS®
SERIES

CHAPTER 4

Should We Militarize Space?

Chapter Preface

From the classic novel *Starship Troopers* to the popular *Star Wars* film franchise, people have long been engaged by fictional accounts of space wars. Many readers and movie buffs might be surprised to learn that space wars aren't entirely fictional. At least so far, however, the role of space in the fighting of wars has been less cinematic, though possibly no less dramatic. In one of this chapter's viewpoints, the author explains that the US military has used satellites for many years to help fight ground wars in places like Iraq and Afghanistan. During this time, the United States was far ahead of the rest of the world in this area. In fact, this technical expertise was one of the country's primary advantages in the wars of the last two decades. In recent years, however, that edge is being threatened. Other nations, such as Russia and China, are developing the ability to deploy anti-satellite weapons. In the United States, this has resulted in calls for more attention to space defense. In 2018, President Donald Trump proposed adding a new branch to the military. This "space force" would be separate from the Air Force, the military branch currently responsible for space. The idea was not new, but up to then it had not gained much traction. When Trump and Vice President Mike Pence publicly endorsed the idea, it suddenly seemed as if a US space force might become a reality. The response was mixed, though, even within the Trump administration. Both Trump's Secretary of Defense and the Secretary of the Air Force thought increasing funding for the Air Force would be a more effective strategy, since the Air Force is already attending to these matters.

Some people objected for more ominous reasons. Virtually everyone agrees that quietly upping the nation's space defenses is long overdue. However, a bold announcement of a new military branch presumably designed to fight wars in space could backfire in many ways, not the least of which would be to provoke enemies to attack satellites before sufficient defenses are in place. Even more likely is the possibility that the plan would launch another arms race that could drain the economy and move the world ever closer to World War III.

In this chapter, we will explore a variety of viewpoints, all of which look at the pros and cons—some focusing more on the pros, some more on the cons—of establishing in the United States a dedicated space force.

"There's nothing we do today, there's not a sailor, soldier, or marine that operates in their domain that isn't using space capabilities to conduct their mission."

We Already Have Militarized Space

Jay Bennett

When we think of militarizing space, most of us imagine something like the Death Star from the Star Wars *movies. In the following viewpoint, Jay Bennett argues that the truth is a little more subtle, though not necessarily any less frightening. As satellites become more essential to waging war on the planet's surface and more rockets, both private and military, are launched into space, the need for protection and the risk of conflicts increase. The author discusses the complications and challenges of space war. Bennett is a former editor for* Popular Mechanics *and now is associate editor at* Smithsonian *magazine.*

"Space War: How the Air Force Plans to Defend the Final Frontier," November 7, 2017. Previously published by *Popular Mechanics*. Reprinted with permission of Hearst Communications, Inc. Written by Jay Bennett.

As you read, consider the following questions:

1. How did the military use satellites in Operation Desert Storm according to the viewpoint?
2. How might the use of satellites and similar technologies change the way wars are fought?
3. Why would the increasingly crowded nature of space add to the risk of international conflicts?

If you ask the Pentagon, the first space war was more than 25 years ago.

"People reference Desert Storm as the first space war," General John W. "Jay" Raymond, commander of Air Force Space Command (AFSPC), said during a recent visit to the Popular Mechanics offices in New York. "It really was the first time that we took strategic space information and integrated it into a theater of operations."

The "left hook" of Operation Desert Storm, when US and allied ground forces attacked the western flank of the Iraqi military in Kuwait, revealed the true power of satellites in wartime. "Going through a desert, at night, without roads and maps—it was all enabled by GPS," Raymond says.

Fast-forward a quarter-century and tensions are again on the rise, from Syria to the Korean Peninsula. And today, the United States no longer enjoys the type of control it had over space in 1991. A hypothetical attack on US satellites has been a serious public concern since at least January 2007, when a Chinese missile shot a Chinese satellite out of the sky. Russia has been researching anti-satellite weapons since at least the 1980s.

The past few decades have shown how space operations can revolutionize military operations on Earth. The next theater, however, might be space itself.

"Both [Russia and China] will continue to pursue a full range of anti-satellite (ASAT) weapons as a means to reduce US military effectiveness," said Daniel Coats, Director of National Intelligence, in a congressional testimony released in May. Last week, Republican

Sen. Jim Inhofe of Oklahoma put it another way while questioning the nominee for NASA Administrator, Jim Bridenstine. "We are in the most threatened position in the history of the country," the senator warned.

The rhetoric coming out of Washington can make it seem as though we are headed into a future of astronaut grunts and laser guns and space shuttle door gunners. A group of congressional leaders have even pushed for legislation to create a new branch of the military: the Space Corps. However, Gen. Raymond paints a slightly different picture of military operations in orbit and the role of American leadership in space.

How We Got Here

Back in 1991, as US troops slogged through the deserts of Kuwait, Saudi Arabia and Iraq, it wasn't just GPS navigation that helped bring swift victory to American forces. One of the most effective weapons the Iraqis had during the Gulf War, Soviet-built Scud missiles, were rendered nearly useless by infrared missile-warning satellites.

While many of America's guided missiles used infrared tracking in the 1990s, "today every weapon we're employing in Iraq and Syria is a precision weapon, and the vast majority are GPS-enabled ones," Raymond says. More than ever, the armed forces are augmented by orbital eyes in the sky.

"There's nothing we do today, there's not a sailor, soldier, or marine that operates in their domain that isn't using space capabilities to conduct their mission," says Raymond. Perhaps the most direct example of space assisting ground forces is the Android Tactical Assault Kit (ATAK), a smartphone that many troops carry on their chests to navigate terrain with GPS, coordinate strikes, set drop and evacuation zones, and generally stay in sync with friendly forces using satellite-enabled capabilities.

To make all that possible, Air Force Space Command operates roughly 80 satellites. You might not know it, but AFSPC is the group that makes sure Google Maps works on your phone. The command operates all 24 to 33 satellites in the GPS constellation for the entire world (though China is working to build their own GPS network of 30 satellites). AFSPC also tracks 23,000 objects in orbit, 1,400 of which are active satellites, using ground-based radar. If the space command detects a possible collision, they notify the satellite owners, regardless of what country or company the satellite belongs to.

America's increasing reliance on those satellites makes them a ripe target for a potential adversary. The United States has enjoyed essentially unchecked control of orbital domains for almost half a century, and while other nations are catching up, US military leaders intend to maintain that control. "Space is foundational to our way of war," says Raymond, "and it's foundational to our way of life."

Stopping a Space Attack

How do you stop another powerful country from taking out your satellites?

"There are vast ways," says Raymond, "and I won't get into the operational details of what we may or may not be able to do, but we're working on being able to protect and defend capabilities from everything from low-end reversible jamming all the way up to the higher-end kinetic activities."

"Kinetic" is the military's favorite euphemism for lethal force via missiles, bullets and the like. In this case, it means destroying a satellite with a weapon that physically smashes into it. Whether the US or other countries are planning to put weapons in orbit—either to kill other satellites or to strike the ground—is classified information. When asked about weapons in space, Raymond simply said, "I'm not going to talk about that." Given the stakes, it's safe to assume that such capabilities are being discussed if not already designed.

But kinetic operations are only a small part of military deterrence. Arguably the most crucial capability, particularly in orbit, is simply knowing where everything is and what it's doing.

"We have four geosynchronous space situational awareness program satellites that actually drift just below the geo belt, kind of the neighborhood watch for space," the general says. These sats augment the ground-based radar that AFSPC uses to track objects in orbit, giving the space command a comprehensive picture of what's going on beyond the reaches of the atmosphere.

AFSPC also gets an assist from one of the United States' premier spy institutions, the National Reconnaissance Office. "We work very closely with the National Reconnaissance Office," Raymond says. "It's our strongest partner." The Air Force is working along with the spy agency to develop a fleet of spacecraft by 2030 that could detect and deter threats, and if necessary, take them out. Information is key, as whichever country has the most complete picture of orbit will likely control the domain.

Guarding America's space assets against attack is a relatively new frontier for the Pentagon. Arguably, however, the more mundane part of the mission is the most important. That is: coordinating the trajectories of tens of thousands of objects encircling the planet in an increasingly crowded and dangerous space.

Space Traffic Control

To defend American spacecraft in orbit, Air Force Space Command often finds itself in the curious position of helping other countries to prevent collisions. "About once every three days a satellite maneuvers to keep from hitting something," Raymond says. "About three times a year the International Space Station maneuvers to keep from hitting debris."

In a worst case scenario, colliding spacecraft could break apart into a debris shower that starts a chain reaction, striking additional spacecraft until you've got a field of swirling metal obstacles. Such a situation would be just as detrimental to US space capabilities as a Chinese missile, if not more so.

"We act as the space traffic control for the world," says Raymond. "It's not in anybody's best interest to have large debris fields."

Space traffic control is getting more challenging. Launch costs continue to fall, space is more crowded than ever, and many satellite operators are using numerous small satellites, such as CubeSats, to replace the bigger, multi-purpose satellites that were prioritized in the past. The variable mission of AFSPC becomes a balancing act between defense—supporting US warfighters with information from orbit—and safeguarding the planet's congested orbital planes so space remains free and open to exploration and scientific research.

Orbit Gets Busy

As for launching its own equipment into orbit, AFSPC plans to expand cooperation with private spaceflight companies. SpaceX in particular has impressed Gen. Raymond. It's not just rocket reusability that drives down costs, he says, but also the autonomous capabilities that SpaceX has built into the Falcon 9 launch vehicle.

"They've built autonomy into their rockets," says Raymond of SpaceX. In the past, a range operator would need to monitor telemetry and radar data from the ground and blow the rocket manually if it went off course. "With SpaceX now... if that launch vehicle launches and it starts to go astray, it senses itself that it's gone past the point where it could impact safety and it blows itself up."

Thanks to new technologies from companies like SpaceX, more rockets will be launched in the coming years than at any other point in history. Earth's orbits will be filled with imaging satellites and broadband satellites and weather satellites and science experiments and whatever else people dream up to send to space. Air Force Space Command, the orbital police, if there is one, is busy preparing for this inevitability.

> *"Article IV of the Outer Space Treaty expresses a principle of use of space for 'peaceful purposes'. ... Military bases, installations and fortifications, weapons testing and conduct of military manouevers on celestial bodies are also forbidden."*

A Space Force Would Violate the Principle of Peaceful Use of Space

Melissa de Zwart

Space may already be militarized, but some feel that dedicating an entire branch of the military to space is necessary to protect US interests there. In the following viewpoint Melissa de Zwart argues that the language Trump used when announcing that he was requesting that Congress establish a space force was quite militaristic. For example, the president used the phrase "new war fighting-domain." This contradicts the spirit, if not the law, of the 1967 Outer Space treaty, which sought to confine the realm of outer space to peaceful uses. de Zwart is dean of Adelaide Law School in Australia and a recognized expert on legal issues surrounding digital technology.

"It's Not Clear Where Trump's 'Space Force' Fits Within International Agreement on Peaceful Use of Space," by Melissa de Zwart, The Conversation, June 19, 2018. https://theconversation.com/its-not-clear-where-trumps-space-force-fits-within-international -agreement-on-peaceful-use-of-space-98545. Licensed under CC BY-ND 4.0 International.

As you read, consider the following questions:

1. What do you think President Trump meant by the statement, "Rich guys seem to like rockets?" and how do you think that influences the push for a space force?
2. Do you think that the president's comments contradict the Outer Space Treaty cited here? Why or why not?
3. What is "A Day without Space," and why do you think it is a routine military exercise?

Overnight US President Donald Trump announced the establishment of a "Space Force" as a separate force of the US military.

Trump has indicated the reasoning behind the Space Force stems from national security concerns arising from the potential for renewed activities in space by China and Russia. Trump had previously referred to space as the "new warfighting domain."

It's not yet clear where this move sits in light of prohibitions laid out in the Outer Space Treaty, the document that has guided the the exploration and use of outer space by members of the United Nations since 1967.

In his recent announcement, Trump said:

> When it comes to defending America, it is not enough to merely have an American presence in space. We must have American dominance in space. So important.

It's Been Coming

Departments in the US military currently include the Air Force, the Army, the Navy, the Marine Corps and the Coast Guard.

The announcement of a Space Force is part of Trump's increased interest in the space domain, having in 2017 revived the National Space Council, under the leadership of Mike Pence.

Trump had previously flagged the idea of a US Space Force with statements in March and May.

However, with this most recent announcement Trump officially directed the US Department of Defense and the Pentagon to establish the Space Force.

Much more will be needed to actually make this happen. The President cannot simply declare the existence of a new branch of the US armed forces—it would also require, at minimum, an Act of Congress and quite possibly something more. Each branch of the US military has its own unique origins and would require the restructure of the Air Force and other oversight mechanisms in the Pentagon.

Further, there is also the question regarding what such a force could do. Trump's speech flagged some sort of peacekeeping role.

Rich Guys Like Rockets

Whilst much of the reportage of Trump's speech has focused on the military aspects of his announcement, Trump reminded the audience that the Space Force was not the only space activity planned by his administration. Rather there was a strong emphasis on commercial space industries, observing that "rich guys seem to like rockets."

US laws relating to commercial space are to be updated to encourage commercial space industries, directing government and the private sector to work cooperatively. Trump said:

> I am instructing my administration to embrace the budding commercial space industry. We are modernizing out-of-date space regulations. They're way out of date. They haven't been changed in many, many years. And today we're taking one more step to unleash the power of American ingenuity. In a few moments, I will sign a new directive to federal departments and agencies. They will work together with American industry to implement a state-of-the-art framework for space traffic management.

Trump also celebrated the potential for benefit to US workers, along with a lot of rhetoric about conquering the unknown. He said "we are Americans and the future belongs totally to us," we will be "leading humanity beyond the Earth" and "into the forbidden skies."

Noting the interest of private entrepreneurs establishing long-term settlements on Mars, Trump observed that whoever made it to Mars first was fine as long as it was a US citizen.

The Outer Space Treaty

Trump's proposals—as with any other new outer space settlements —must operate within prohibitions laid out in the Outer Space Treaty. Established in 1967, this document is the framework multilateral treaty that establishes the principal rules regulating the exploration and use of outer space.

Article II of the Outer Space Treaty indicates that "Outer space, including the moon and other celestial bodies, is not subject to national appropriation by claim of sovereignty, by means of use or occupation, or by any other means."

That said, US law has been drafted to enable access to, including mining of, space resources, without any claim of sovereignty being made.

With respect to a Space Force, Article IV of the Outer Space Treaty expresses a principle of use of space for "peaceful purposes." Members of the Outer Space Treaty are forbidden from placing nuclear weapons or weapons of mass destruction in orbit around the Earth, on celestial bodies or stationed in outer space. Military bases, installations and fortifications, weapons testing and conduct of military manouevers on celestial bodies are also forbidden.

Of course, none of this has prevented military personnel being involved in space activities and exploration since the dawn of the space age. Both the early US astronauts and Soviet cosmonauts have been members of their respective countries armed forces. Nor has it prevented the transit of weapons of mass destruction through space. GPS is a development of the US Department of Defense and many satellites, including Australia's own Optus C1 satellite is a dual use (military and civilian) satellite.

All Eyes on Space

The question of the legality of the extent of military uses of outer space and what role may be performed by Trump's Space Force is still open.

Generally, the practice of the space faring states to date indicates that the prohibitions contained in Article IV of the Outer Space Treaty have been interpreted as "peaceful," but as referring to non-aggressive rather than non-military uses of space.

Of course, militaries worldwide are already very reliant upon space in terms of communication, position, navigation and timing, surveillance and reconnaissance. Militaries regularly hold exercises such as a Day without Space, which prepares users for the possible destruction of or serious interference with GPS, internet and satellites communications, upon which all modern militaries are heavily reliant.

Space assets such as satellites are quite fragile and valuable and hence issues will inevitably arise regarding capacity to protect space assets.

Trump's Space Force may still be a highly speculative announcement but it is true that we live in an era where militaries and civilians worldwide are becoming far more reliant and invested in the space domain.

> "What the military does need . . . is to create career paths for people who specialize in space. To stay ahead over the next half-century, the United States needs to 'grow the space leaders.'"

We Don't Need a Space Force

Joe Pappalardo

In 2018, US president Donald Trump proposed the addition of a branch of the nation's military, a space force, not a new idea, but one that had never gotten so far as an endorsement from a president. Many science fiction fans were delighted, but the idea faced a great deal of resistance, even from Trump's own Secretary of Defense. In the following viewpoint, Joe Pappalardo speaks with military leaders about the concept of a military force in space. Those interviewed explain that the United States does indeed need more money and innovative approaches to protecting space technologies, but it probably does not need a dedicated space force. Pappalardo is contributing editor at Popular Mechanics. *His work has appeared on CNN, MSNBC, Fox News, and Esquire.com, among other media outlets.*

"Why Would We Need a U.S. Space Force, Anyway?" June 19, 2018. Previously published by *Popular Mechanics* magazine. Reprinted with permission of Hearst Communications, Inc. Written by Joe Pappalardo.

As you read, consider the following questions:

1. Why does the US need to up its game regarding space defense according to this viewpoint?
2. What effect would the establishment of a space force as an additional branch of the military have on private defense contractors?
3. How do the sources quoted by the author say that the proposed budget for a space force fail to meet the particular needs of the military's space initiatives?

The idea of the space force is nothing new. Just this year the House of Representatives tried to create a sixth branch of the military in the 2018 National Defense Authorization Act, but the plan died in the Senate. Yesterday, however, Trump revived these hopes. "We have the Air Force, we'll have the Space Force," he said at a Marine Corps airbase.

The Air Force, which runs most of America's space-related defense activities, is strongly opposed to the Space Force. And there are plenty of hurdles to clear, political and otherwise, before the United States comes close to realizing a real Space Force.

What's more interesting is why America needs a space force in the first place. The answers to that question emerged from a House of Representatives meeting in the wake of Trump's announcement, in which space war experts tore into the issue before the House Armed Services Committee.

Why a Space Force?

"When I was head of STRATCOM I thought I was commanding the US space forces," said Air Force Gen. Robert Kehler (ret.), the former commander of US Strategic Command. Like many who come from USAF, he's lukewarm on the idea of a Space Force. (The Secretary of the Air Force sidestepped questions about Trump in a separate meeting yesterday.) But he reiterated to the committee that the US military must change its mindset about space.

PROTECTION FROM A DIFFERENT KIND OF SPACE THREAT

If a dangerous asteroid appears to be on a collision course for Earth, one option is to send a spacecraft to destroy it with a nuclear warhead. Such a mission, which would cost about $1 billion, could be developed from work NASA is already funding, a prominent asteroid defense expert says.

Bong Wie, director of the Asteroid Deflection Research Center at Iowa State University, described the system his team is developing to attendees at the International Space Development Conference in La Jolla, Calif., on May 23. The annual National Space Society gathering attracted hundreds from the space industry around the world.

An anti-asteroid spacecraft would deliver a nuclear warhead to destroy an incoming threat before it could reach Earth, Wie said. The two-section spacecraft would consist of a kinetic energy impactor that would separate before arrival and blast a crater in the asteroid. The other half of the spacecraft would carry the nuclear weapon, which would then explode inside the crater after the vehicle impacted.

The goal would be to fragment the asteroid into many pieces, which would then disperse along separate trajectories. Wie believes that up to 99 percent or more of the asteroid pieces could end up missing the Earth, greatly limiting the impact on the planet. Of those that do reach our world, many would burn up in the atmosphere and pose no threat.

Wie's study has focused on providing the capability to respond to a threatening asteroid on short notices of a year or so. The plan would be to have two spacecraft on standby—one primary, the other backup—that could be launched on Delta 4 rockets. If the first spacecraft failed on launch or didn't fragment the asteroid, the second would be sent aloft to finish the job.

"Nuking Dangerous Asteroids Might Be the Best Protection, Expert Says," by Douglas Messie, Space.com, May 29, 2013.

American forces must "gain and maintain space superiority" as a condition for fighting, he said. This echoes the way the USAF first gains control of the airspace above before engaging in a ground campaign.

One reason that superiority may erode is that disparate space-related efforts are scattered across the Army, Air Force, and Navy, not to mention intelligence officers, National Reconnaissance Office and Space and Missile Systems Center. Doug Loverro, a former DoD Deputy Assistant Secretary of Defense for Space Policy, noted that fighting in space is different than fighting anywhere else, in the same way that the Navy prepares for unique combat at sea. "We lack that focus for space, one of our five main warfighting domains," he said.

Loverro joked that people have been blaming him for Trump's endorsement of a new service. "I'm ready to rip the band aid off," he said. Yet even he concedes a new service may not be needed. "We don't need to move it from the USAF to create the space smart-force we need," he said.

What the military does need, he said, is to create career paths for people who specialize in space. To stay ahead over the next half-century, the United States needs to "grow the space leaders." He compared the foundation of the US Air Force, which guaranteed the expertise in personnel, led to the United States' dominance in the air. "The same will be true for space," he said.

Todd Harrison, Director of Aerospace Security Project, Center for Strategic and International Studies, advocated for "a dedicated cadre of space acquisition professionals" who can take advantage of the "renaissance" sweeping the commercial space industry. He also suggested creating a capitol fund for rapid response and prototyping for space systems. "We have to evolve our thinking over time, and I think we've reached that point," Harrison said. "It's time to rethink our organizational thinking."

Promise v. Reality

While the warfighting plans reflect the realities of space conflict, Kehler said, the Pentagon's space weapons strategy can't catch up with the pace of the growing threats.

In 2016 the Pentagon released its Space Enterprise Vision, heralded as a new direction to elevate space in the eyes of the

USAF. The document reads well, but Loverro said "The budget doesn't reflect that vision."

For example, Loverro noted a lack of tests or exercises dedicated to space war, especially ones that include allies, which is something the US does consistently for air combat. Even worse, the funding supports "old school space architectures" like large satellites that are easier targets for adversaries, as opposed to using several smaller sats.

These threats, Loverro said, are already here. If a war broke out in the Pacific, commanders would have a hard time communicating with troops. "We have a SATCOM jamming threat today," Loverro told Congress. "We have nothing on books until 2027 to solve that problem."

He also cited institutional thinking as a constraint. The legendary scientist Johannes Kepler said there are infinite orbits to choose from, but only four are used. "We are not constrained by gravity or physics, but culturally we have a hard time moving away from them," Loverro said. "It is convenient to be in geostationary orbit, but it is not militarily wise to be in geostationary orbit."

Gen. Kehler said the stakes are high because the loss of critical assets in space could prove decisive in a future battle. Potential enemies know this and have been investing in weapons on the ground or in space to take out or jam satellites. "Time is not on our side," he said.

Update 6/19/18: At a meeting of the National Space Council in Washington D.C. on Monday, June 18th, President Trump called on the Pentagon to create a space force, saying "I am hereby directing the Department of Defense and Pentagon to immediately begin the process necessary to establish a Space Force as the sixth branch of the armed forces." While the Pentagon can create a plan for a space force, the power to finalize such an organization and to fund it ultimately falls with Congress.

> *"Allies and adversaries alike would see putting interceptors in space as the first time anyone's put dedicated destructive weapons up there. If you're concerned about keeping space secure and usable, it would be crossing a line."*

A US Space Force Could Set Off a Dangerous Arms Race

Paul March-Russell

In the following viewpoint Paul March-Russell argues that President Trump's announcement of a space military harkens back to the Reagan administration's Strategic Defense Initiative. The similarity, he claims, is in the attempt of both to convince the public of a potential threat that only can be solved with American military force and the promise of expansion. However, he concedes, Trump's plans probably are more likely to go nowhere. March-Russell is a lecturer in Comparative Literature at the University of Kent, with a special focus on science fiction.

"Donald Trump's Space Force Plans Analysed by a Sci-Fi Expert," by Paul March-Russell, The Conversation, August 16, 2018. https://theconversation.com/donald-trumps -space-force-plans-analysed-by-a-sci-fi-expert-101549. Licensed Under CC BY-ND 4.0 International.

As you read, consider the following questions:

1. Why does the author state that Trump's proposal for a space force is specifically like American science fiction as opposed to sci-fi from other countries?
2. By what nickname was President Ronald Reagan's Strategic Defense Initiative (SDI) known?
3. Why does the author call Trump's plan a "reboot"?

The US leadership has plans to introduce a "US Space Force" by 2020. Already announced by president Donald Trump in June, US vice president Mike Pence outlined further details of the plan at a press conference on August 9. The Space Force, he said, would consist of an elite corps of soldiers trained to fight in space, and a space command that would design military strategies for warfare beyond the atmosphere.

Much acrimony and ridicule has ensued, with debates over what such a force could or could not do; the only certainty being that it will cost billions of dollars. Seasoned watchers of both US politics and US science fiction will have had the uncanny feeling, though, of having seen this all before.

The rhetoric of both Pence and Trump, referring respectively to "the boundless expanse of space" and the necessity for "American dominance", is inherently science-fictional, but of a particularly American kind. It is not the cooperatist vision of Soviet science fiction, nor the ramshackled approach of British sci-fi (take *Doctor Who*), and certainly not the Afrofuturist marriage of esoteric technology and indigenous folklore, seen most recently in Ava DuVernay's *A Wrinkle in Time*.

An American Fiction

Instead, it is the projection of the values of Manifest Destiny (that the settler population has an inalienable right to the uncharted lands) into outer space. Not for nothing did Trump's 2020 reelection campaign manager, Brad Parscale, write that the Space Force would be "a groundbreaking endeavor for America and the final frontier."

As film and media studies expert, Constance Penley, observed in her 1997 book, *NASA/Trek*, the Cold War politics of the Space Race dovetailed beautifully with the frontier vision of Gene Roddenberry's *Star Trek*. This is particularly true of the pioneer spirit of (to paraphrase the original series' opening words) exploring "strange new worlds," seeking "out new life and new civilisations," and "boldly" going "where no man has gone before."

Roddenberry himself was in a lineage of writers from Edgar Rice Burroughs to Ray Bradbury who, with varying degrees of scepticism, projected frontier values into outer space (most typically, onto the surface of Mars). And as historian Frederic Krome has shown, future war stories published in the US pulps between 1914 and 1945 fed into the cultural and military thinking of how to plan for future conflicts.

Perhaps most bizarrely, the mission to capture Saddam Hussein during the Iraq War was named after John Milius's post-apocalyptic teen movie, *Red Dawn* (1984).

Indeed, the Strategic Defence Initiative (SDI), envisaged by president Ronald Reagan in 1983, not only became known as "Star Wars," but its rhetoric was also derived from science fiction writers such as Ben Bova and Jerry Pournelle. SDI's vision of a circling belt of laser-armed satellites, protecting the US from Soviet attack, chimed perfectly with Pournelle's dream, and with that of other science fiction writers such as Robert Heinlein and Larry Niven—an American renaissance through the militarisation and colonisation of space.

Space Force Rebooted

The current rhetoric of Pence and Trump, in announcing their Space Force, almost exactly echoes the rhetoric of SDI and its then supporters. Both groups posit a pattern of US military decline, under the alleged negligence of previous administrations, in which space, the "natural" home of the US following the moon landings, has been left exposed to foreign aggressors. According to them, it is their enemies, not the US, who have militarised space. And now, they argue, only a show of strength can make space safe again for US democracy.

In this way, the ratcheting-up of an arms race in space is glossed over by a utopian vision, in which the US is regalvanised by dreams of expansion into space—see, for example, the proposed mission to Mars.

There has been genuine concern since 2007, when China shot down one of its own satellites. But to imply that space has only now begun to be militarised glosses over the steady militarisation of space since the 1960s, while even supporters of the proposal suggest a cyber-hacking force is more necessary.

Instead, the proposal for an elite corps of specialised soldiers and strategists sounds more like Heinlein's controversial novel of a fully militarised society, *Starship Troopers* (1959), in which humans are embroiled in a seemingly endless war against the utterly alien "Bugs." There are echoes too of E E Smith's interstellar police force, *Galactic Patrol* (1937), and even the BBC's more low-key *Star Cops* (1987), glumly policing off-world mining colonies in the outer solar system. Of course, the proposal may never take flight—it would still require an Act of Congress—so these more hyperbolic fears and desires may need to be momentarily put aside.

Instead, what we can deduce from the proposal is that we are firmly in the logic of the reboot, that much loved tactic of longrunning movie franchises. But, as science fiction scholar Gerry Canavan has argued, the reboot "can show us a story, but can't tell us a plot." Rather than an original and inspiring vision of space exploration, what we have instead here is a meaningless reiteration of past rhetoric that may, quite literally, go nowhere.

> "[The Outer Space Treaty] ... doesn't explicitly forbid intercontinental ballistic missiles, which enter and exit space on their way toward their targets.

A Space Force Might Not Be Legal

Michael Greshko

While many are questioning the necessity and prudence of a space force as a sixth military branch, others are wondering if such a project would even be legal under international law. In the following viewpoint, Michael Greshko answers a series of basic questions about what exactly is being proposed and what it would and would not do. The question of whether or not it would be legal is perhaps the most complex of the lot. Greshko is a science writer at National Geographic.

As you read, consider the following questions:

1. What branch of the US government has the authority to create a new military branch?
2. Why are so many current and former military personnel and advisors opposed to the idea of a space force?
3. What do international treaties say about what can and cannot be done in space?

"Would a U.S. Space Force Be Legal? Get the Facts," by Michael Greshko, National Geographic Society, August 9, 2018. Reprinted by permission.

I n a speech at the Pentagon on Thursday, US Vice President Mike Pence announced more details for a Space Force: a proposed sixth branch of the US military that would focus on all matters off-world, from procuring military satellites to defending US spacecraft in orbit from attacks.

"Just as in the past, when we created the Air Force, establishing the Space Force is an idea whose time has come," Pence said. "The space environment has fundamentally changed in the last generation; what was once peaceful and uncontested is now crowded and adversarial."

Pence's speech rekindles a news cycle that, at first glance, resembles the prologue of a sci-fi film. In June, US President Donald Trump made international headlines by voicing support for a Space Force in remarks to the National Space Council.

"I'm hereby directing the Department of Defense and Pentagon to immediately begin the process necessary to establish a space force as the sixth branch of the armed forces. That's a big statement," Trump said. "We are going to have the Air Force and we are going to have the Space Force—separate but equal."

In the wake of Pence's speech and Trump's directive, you may have some questions. Does the US now have starship troopers? What are the pros and cons to a Space Force? And is such a military branch even legal under international treaties? We've got you covered.

Does the US Now Have a Space Force?

Not yet. Only an act of Congress can create a new military branch, but the Trump Administration is sketching out how one would work. If Congress assents, the branch would be the first added to the US military since 1947, when the Air Force was founded.

President Trump has entertained the notion of space warriors before, first in a March 2018 speech and later in a May 2018 Rose Garden ceremony. But just last year, his Cabinet opposed the idea.

"The Pentagon is complicated enough," Air Force Secretary Heather Wilson told reporters in June 2017. "This will make it more complex, add more boxes to the organization chart, and cost more money. If I had more money, I would put it into lethality, not bureaucracy."

In July 2017, Secretary of Defense Jim Mattis even wrote to Congress to speak out against a Space Corps proposal, one that lawmakers eventually scrapped. The idea still has its supporters inside and outside Congress, who argue that space is now too important to lack a dedicated military branch.

"Space is a place where there is now tens of billions of dollars" in infrastructure, says Mark Albrecht, the executive secretary of the National Space Council from 1989 to 1992. "Everything from financial transactions to the GPS that guides your car is controlled from space, or at least facilitated by space."

Military activity in space, he argues, is therefore "not materially different from the US Navy, which goes around the Pacific and the Atlantic and the Mediterranean not to create trouble or to cause wars, but to make sure that all the things we enjoy are protected."

The US military depends heavily on space for communications, reconnaissance, and detecting incoming missiles. Russia and China have been building surface-to-air missiles powerful enough to take out a satellite, Albrecht notes, a move that has US officials increasingly concerned. In 2007, China even shot down one of its own aging weather satellites in a test of the technology that the US protested.

In the 2018 National Defense Authorization Act, Congress directed the Pentagon to at least study if and how it should reorganize its existing space programs. An interim version of the study, published in March, and it is noncommittal to the idea of what was then called a unified "Space Corps." Defense One reports that the full study calls for consolidating the US military's space operations. The plan is to establish a US Space Command akin to the cross-cutting US Indo-Pacific Command, and to craft a single agency that would buy the military's satellites.

"Before Congress does anything, I think they're going to want to see that report and see what the Department of Defense says about that," says Michael Dodge, a space law expert at the University of North Dakota's Department of Space Studies.

Is a Space Force a Totally New Proposal?

No. The idea of a Space Force has been kicked around for decades. In a 1999 policy paper, Senator Bob Smith entertained the idea, and the following year, a commission chaired by Donald Rumsfeld suggested making a Space Corps within the Air Force, an analogue to the Marine Corps within the US Navy.

From Eisenhower to Obama, the US has seen space as a zone for self-defense and non-aggressive military activities. But by advocating for a Space Force, observers say that Trump is taking an unusually brazen tack.

"It sends a message to other countries around the world that the US is looking aggressively at our future in space with respect to national defense," says Dodge. "What I mean by 'aggressively' is the signaling that the US is looking at space as a potential war-fighting domain—which is nothing new, but probably isn't helpful to discourse."

What Would a Space Force Actually Look Like?

In all likelihood, a Space Force would be stitched together from existing US programs. At its center would be the Air Force Space Command, which has led the US's military space operations since 1982.

If you're picturing a rehash of *Starship Troopers* or *The Expanse*, brace yourself for disappointment. Day to day, the Space Force would probably monitor Earth's satellites and take the lead on launching and maintaining military satellites, the command's current beat.

Even now, the command employs more than 36,000 people and maintains military tech in space, such as the Global Positioning System (GPS) satellite network and the mysterious X-37B space plane. The consulting firm Avascent says that the Air Force spends more than $7 billion per year on unclassified space systems alone.

At its most elaborate, a Space Force would be on equal footing with the Army and Navy, replete with Pentagon offices and a service academy like West Point. However, its exact structure would depend on the enacting laws, which aren't passing any time soon.

Albrecht estimates that at the absolute fastest, it'd take at least a year to make the Space Force a legal entity. In his August 9 speech, Vice President Pence said that officials are optimistic a Space Force could blast off as soon as 2020.

Costs for the branch would vary, depending on how it was organized. In an interview with the *Washington Post*, National Space Council executive secretary Scott Pace said that the Trump Administration's proposed reorganization "should be budget neutral." The *Post* also noted that the White House has asked Congress for an extra $8 billion over the next five years to bolster funding for national security systems in space.

Would Military Action in Space Be Legal?

In a word, yes. But if a US Space Force ever came online, legal experts say that international law would limit what it could do.

All major space powers, including the US, Russia, and China, have signed the Outer Space Treaty of 1967. The pact says that nothing in space can be claimed as a single country's territory, and it bars countries from stationing nuclear weapons or weapons of mass destruction anywhere in outer space, including in orbit around Earth.

The treaty gets stricter when it comes to "celestial bodies" such as the moon and Mars. Parties can't build military bases, conduct military maneuvers, or test weapons of any kind—even conventional weapons—on another world.

But the Outer Space Treaty does give countries some wiggle room. Dodge says that the Cold War-era treaty doesn't explicitly forbid intercontinental ballistic missiles, which enter and exit space on their way toward their targets. The treaty also doesn't specify whether conventional weapons can be used in open space or on space stations. And they have, at least once: In January 1975, the

Soviet Union secretly test-fired a modified cannon on its Almaz space station.

"I don't think that necessarily would have violated the treaty, even if it's contrary to the spirit of the document itself," says Dodge.

That said, the Outer Space Treaty and other space treaties aren't the only rules in the void.

"Space is like the high seas, it's like Antarctica—it's a global commons. And that means it's governed by international law," says Joanne Gabrynowicz, a space law expert and professor emerita at the University of Mississippi. "In addition to the Outer Space Treaty, the whole body of international law applies to space, and that includes humanitarian law [such as the Geneva Conventions] and the law of armed conflict."

Gabrynowicz adds that even the proposed branch's name could raise legal questions.

"There's a term of art in law called the 'use of force,'" she says, "[and] that phrase has a huge body of law just on what that means."

Periodical and Internet Sources Bibliography

*The following articles have been selected to supplement the diverse
views presented in this chapter.*

Ann Deslandes, "The Bold Future of the Outer Space Treaty: With
President Trump calling for a 'Space Force' and private enterprise
increasingly invested in space, what of the dream of international
peace?" JSTOR Daily, August 1, 2018. https://daily.jstor.org/the
-bold-future-of-the-outer-space-treaty/.

Mary Beth Griggs, "Trump's Space Force Could Be One Giant Leap
into a Tricky Situation," *Popular Science*, June 19. https://www
.popsci.com/trump-military-space-force.

Fred Kaplan, "Space Farce: Space defense will be a major concern for
the U.S., but Trump's 'Space Force' is not the answer," Slate, June
21, 2018. https://slate.com/news-and-politics/2018/06/trumps
-space-force-idea-is-a-terrible-solution-to-a-real-problem.html.

Jeffrey Kluger, "Why Trump's 'Space Force' Won't—and shouldn't—
Happen," *Time*, June 19, 2018. http://time.com/5316007/space
-force-trump.

Bob McDonald, "Trump's 'Dominance' in Space is Playing with
International Space Treaty," CBC Radio, June 22, 2018. https://
www.cbc.ca/radio/quirks/blog/trump-s-dominance-in-space-is
-playing-with-international-space-treaty-1.4718058.

New York Times Editorial Board, "Trump in Space: The president's
plans for a new military force could spur an extraterrestrial arms
race and make combat in orbit more likely," July 27, 2018. https://
www.nytimes.com/2018/07/27/opinion/trump-space-force
-military.html.

Hope Hodge Seck, "Air Force Issues First Guidance to Troops about
Space Force," military.com, 20 June 2018. https://www.military
.com/daily-news/2018/06/20/air-force-issues-first-guidance
-troops-about-space-force.html.

Amy Thompson, "Did Donald Trump Just Declare Space War?" *The
Observer*, June 20, 2018. https://observer.com/2018/06/trump
-space-force-tests-united-nations-outer-space-treaty.

Loren Thompson, "10 Ways a Space Force Will Make America
Weaker," *Forbes*, August 27, 2018. https://www.forbes.com/sites

/lorenthompson/2018/08/27/ten-ways-a-space-force-will-make
-america-weaker/#2e6d755834b0.

Alex Ward, "Trump's Call for a Space Force, Explained," Vox, updated
March 13, 2018. https://www.vox.com/world/2017/7/5/15905018
/space-force-trump-congress-russia-china.

John Wenz, "The proposed Space Force isn't the first time the United
States has tried to militarize space," *Popular Science*, June 20,
2018. https://www.popsci.com/air-force-space-force.

For Further Discussion

Chapter 1

1. Leigh Cooper writes about about potential moral issues that may arise as a result of space exploration. How do you think these problems would be addressed differently by private companies than by governments? Do you think either would be better suited to deal with these kinds of issues? Explain.
2. In Nadine Cranenburgh's viewpoint, one of her sources argues that outer space should be treated just like international waters when it comes to mining rights and so on. Do you agree? Why or why not? Has this arrangement worked well in Earth?
3. In the last viewpoint in this chapter, Mitchell Gunter points out that private space companies are heavily subsidized by the government. Do you think this is a good way to stimulate innovation? Or is it an unfair use of taxpayer money?

Chapter 2

1. The first viewpoint in this chapter suggests that it might be safer to lie low and hope advanced civilizations never find us. On the other hand, if they are truly advanced, they might be able to help us with some of our pressing problems. If you had to make this decision, what would you do?
2. Marcelo Gleiser makes a convincing case that intelligent life is rare in the universe. Yet many other scientists disagree. Can you find places in his argument where you might challenge his view? For example, might anaerobic life have evolved intelligence as well?
3. Adam Frank mentions silicon as a possible techno-signature. Do you think that searching for techno-signatures, such as

silicon, could lead us to look only for civilizations that are like our own?

Chapter 3

1. In the first viewpoint in this chapter the authors argue that government investment into scientific research is essential to economic growth. Do you think this suggests that the United States is making a mistake by leaving so much modern space exploration in private hands? Why or why not?

2. The viewpoint taken from a NASA publication lists many benefits we take for granted today that came directly from the first fifty years of space exploration. What innovations can you imagine that will come if space exploration is treated as seriously in the next fifty years as it was in the last half of the twentieth century?

3. In the fifth viewpoint in the chapter, we encounter for the second time in this volume a reference to the international division of Antarctica. Do you think that is a good model for the Moon and other space bodies? Why or why not?

Chapter 4

1. Several of the people quoted in this chapter argue that the duties of a proposed space force are best left under the jurisdiction of the Air Force. Do you agree? Why might a military branch that specialized just in space be useful? How might such a proposal backfire?

2. Most of the viewpoints in this chapter agree that there is a need to protect satellites. However, they don't agree on the best way to do that. What do you think are the greatest concerns of those who oppose the establishment of a space force? What are the primary concerns of those who support it?

3. Viewpoint four of this chapter argues that the establishment of a space force might lead to a new arms race. The author

mentions the unfortunate consequences of the bombastic rhetoric of President Ronald Reagan, and suggests that Donald Trump might be making a similar mistake. Can you explain why some experts feel that a subtler approach to defense might be more effective?

Organizations to Contact

The editors have compiled the following list of organizations concerned with the issues debated in this book. The descriptions are derived from materials provided by the organizations. All have publications or information available for interested readers. The list was compiled on the date of publication of the present volume; the information provided here may change. Be aware that many organizations take several weeks or longer to respond to inquiries, so allow as much time as possible.

Australian Space Agency

Industry House
10 Binara Street in the Canberra CBD
Department of Industry, Innovation and Science
GPO 2013, Canberra, ACT, 2601
+61 2 6213 6000
email: enquiry@industry.gov.au
website: industry.gov.au/strategies-for-the-future/australian
-space-agency

The Australian Space Agency is a government agency responsible for coordination of civil space matters and is the primary source of advice to the Australian Government on civil space policy.

Canadian Space Agency

6767 Route de l'Aeroport
Saint-Hubert, Quebec
J3Y 8Y9
(450) 926-4800
email: contact via website
website: asc-csa.gc.ca

The Canadian Space Agency coordinates all government-funded space activities in Canada, including the nation's robotics program.

The Commonwealth Scientific and Industrial Research Organisation (CSIRO)

GPO Box 1700
Canberra ACT 2601
Australia
phone: 1300 363 400
email: CSIROenquires@csiro.au
website: Csiro.au

CSIRO is an independent Australian federal government agency responsible for scientific research, including space related projects such as radio astronomy, spacecraft tracking, and Earth observation and informatics.

European Space Agency (ESA)

ESA HQ Bertrand
24 rue du Général Bertrand
CS 30798
75345 Paris CEDEX 7
France
+33 1 53 69 76 54
website: Esa.int

The ESA is an intergovernmental agency dedicated to cooperation among European States in space research and technology and their space applications for exclusively peaceful purposes, including scientific research.

National Aeronautics and Space Administration (NASA)

NASA Headquarters
300 E. Street SW, Suite 5R30
Washington, DC 20546
(202) 358-0001 (Office)
website: NASA.gov

NASA is an independent agency of the US government responsible for civilian space program and aerospace and aeronautics research.

National Space Society

P.O. Box 98106
Washington, DC 20090-8106
(202) 429-1600
website: space.nss.org

An independent, nonpartisan educational society dedicated to the creation of a spacefaring civilization.

The Planetary Society

60 South Los Robles Avenue
Pasadena, CA 91101
USA
(626) 793-5100
email: tps@planetary.org
website: Planetary.org

The Planetary Society is a nonprofit organization dedicated to advance public knowledge about space science and space exploration.

ROSCOSMOS (State Space Corporation)

42, Schepkina St.
Moscow, Russia, 107996
+7 (495) 660-2323
email: info@roscosmos.ru
website: roscosmos.ru

Roscosmos is the state agency responsible for space flight and aeronautics in the Russian Federation.

Space Frontier Foundation

1900 S. Eads Street, Unit 430
Arlington, VA, 22202
email: info@spacefrontier.org
website: spacefrontier.org

Space Frontier Foundation is an organization committed to realizing the vision of a greatly expanded and permanent human presence in space.

Space Studies Institute

7429 Laurel Canyon Blvd.
North Hollywood, CA 91605
(661) 750-2774
email: admin@ssi.org
website: ssi.org

Space Studies Institute is an organization dedicated to completing the missing technological links to make possible the productive use of the abundant resources in space.

Bibliography of Books

Neil Clarke, ed., *The Final Frontier: Stories of Exploring Space, Colonizing the Universe, and First Contact*, New York, NY: Nightshade, 2018.

Christian Davenport, *The Space Barons: Elon Musk, Jeff Bezos, and the Quest to Colonize the Cosmos*, New York, NY: Public Affairs, 2018.

Michael H. Gorn, *Spacecraft: 100 Iconic Rockets, Shuttles, and Satellites that Put Us in Space*. Minneapolis, MN: Quarto, 2018.

David Grinspoon, *Earth in Human Hands*, New York, NY: Grand Central, 2016.

Julian Guthrie, *How to Make a Spaceship: A Band of Renegades, An Epic Race, and the Birth of Private Spaceflight*, New York, NY: Penguin, 2016.

Roger D. Launius, *The Smithsonian History of Space Exploration: From the Ancient World to the Extraterrestrial Future*. Washington, DC: Smithsonian Books, 2018.

Joe Pappalardo, *Spaceport Earth: The Reinvention of Space Flight*. New York, NY: Overlook, 2017.

Charles Pappas, *One Giant Leap: The Greatest American Space Race Inventions that Changed the World*, Lanham, MD: Lyons, 2019.

Rod Pyle, *Amazing Stories of the Space Age: True Tales of Nazis in Orbit, Soldiers on the Moon, Orphaned Martian Robots, and Other Fascinating Accounts from the Annals of Spaceflight*. Amherst, NY: Prometheus, 2017.

_____. *Space 2.0: How Private Spaceflight, a Resurgent NASA, and International Partners are Creating a New Space Age*. Dallas, TX: BenBella, 2019.

Mary Roach, *Packing for Mars: The Curious Science of Life in the Void*. New York, NY: Norton, 2010.

Carl Sagan, *Contact*, New York, NY: Simon and Schuster, 1997.

Sarah Scoles, *Making Contact: Jill Tarter and the Search for Extraterrestrial Intelligence*, Trenton, TX: Pegasus, 2017.

Lynn Sherr, *Sally Ride: The First Woman in Space*, New York, NY: Simon and Schuster, 2014.

Margo Shetterly, *Hidden Figures: The American Dream and the Untold Story of the Black Women Mathematicians Who Helped Win the Space Race.* New York, NY: William Morrow, 2016.

Alan Stern and David Grinspoon, *Chasing New Horizons: Inside the Epic First Mission to Pluto,* New York, NY: Picador, 2018.

Ashlee Vance, *Elon Musk: Tesla, SpaceX, and the Quest for a Fantastic Future.* New York, NY: Harper Collins, 2015.

Charles Wohlforth, *Beyond Earth: Our Path to a New Home in the Planets,* New York, NY: Pantheon, 2016.

Index

A

Advanced Aerospace Threat Identification Program, 55

Air Force Space Command, 136–139, 157

Allen, Paul, 86

Allen Array, 86

Alpha Centauri, 56, 76

Amazon, 25, 32

American Association for the Advancement of Science, 31, 67

Android Tactical Assault Kit, 136–137

Apollo Space Program, 26, 31, 34, 107–108, 127, 128

Armstrong, Neil, 15

astrobiology, 76, 77, 78

astronauts, 15, 24–25, 27–29, 43, 46, 136, 143

B

Bennett, Jay, 134

Berkeley Search for Extraterrestrial Intelligence Research Center, 55

Bezos, Jeff, 16, 25, 29, 80

bio-signature, 78, 79

black holes, 78, 80

Blue Origin, 24, 25, 44, 46

Bolden, Charles, 46–47

Branson, Richard, 25, 29, 102

Breakthrough Listen, 54–55

C

Chandrayaan-1, 126, 127

China, 16, 26–28, 112–113, 153, 156, 158

Clarke, Arthur C., 72

Cold War (1947–1991), 16, 31, 152, 159

Columbia, 113

Commercial Orbital Transportation Services (COTS), 47

Cooper, Leigh, 30

cosmonauts, 26, 112, 120, 143

Cranenburgh, Nadine, 35

D

Darwin, Charles, 100–101

Defense Advanced Research Projects Agency (DARPA), 107

Department of Defense, 24, 54–55, 107, 117, 142–143, 149, 155, 156–157

Falcon program, 24, 41, 46, 47, 117, 139

De Zwart, Melissa, 140

E

Earth, 15, 20, 23, 25, 27, 29, 31, 36–44, 46–48, 55–57, 66–69, 71, 100–102, 114, 119–123, 126–128, 135, 139, 143

value of, 98–99

Easter Island, 94–95, 101